BROTHERS, WE ARE NOT PLAGIARISTS

A PASTORAL PLEA TO FORSAKE THE
PEDDLING OF GOD'S WORD

DAVID SCHROCK

Brothers, We Are Not Plagiarists:
A Pastoral Plea to Forsake the Peddling of God's Word

©2022 Founders Press

Published by Founders Press
P.O. Box 150931 • Cape Coral, FL • 33915
Phone: (888) 525-1689
Electronic Mail: officeadmin@founders.org
Website: www.founders.org

Printed in the United States of America

ISBN: 978-0-9654955-6-1

Contents

Foreword

In 2 Timothy 2:15, the apostle Paul admonished Timothy, "Do your best to present yourself to God as one approved, a worker who has no need to be ashamed, rightly handling the word of truth." Rightly handling the Word of God—which the man of God is called to preach in the power of the Spirit of God—is inherent in being the kind of worker that God approves. This is the aspiration of every pastor and indeed everyone who is given the responsibility to preach God's Word.

This responsibility is the primary duty of men whom God equips and calls to shepherd his people. The fact that Paul admonishes Timothy to "rightly" handle the Word reminds us that it is very possible to handle Scripture wrongly. Blatant mishandling of Scripture is rather obvious, like the time I heard a man quote "For we wrestle not . . . " (Eph. 6:12a) as his text for a devotional message for a pastors' gathering, and then launch into a tirade on the cowardice of modern preachers because they were afraid to fight!

He may have had a point, but he surely didn't get it from that text.

But Paul's admonition does not only concern faulty exegesis and interpretation (though it most certainly includes that), it also forbids any other shameful tactics that a man who is tasked with preaching might be tempted to employ. Preaching other people's sermons as if they are your own would most definitely be included among such activities. Sadly, in recent years we have witnessed several high-profile examples of pastors taking exact words, jokes, and even personal-life illustrations from other preachers and using them as if they are original. Such pulpit plagiarism is shameful.

Every pastor who gives himself to diligent study in the work of sermon preparation knows what it is to benefit from the insights of scholars, theologians, exegetes, commentators, and other preachers. We want to do our best to make sure we understand the text we are preparing to preach and we also want to preach it in the very best way possible. Those noble aspirations, however, can yield to subtle temptations to take the work of others and simply parrot it as if it is our own.

At most points, knowing where careful research ends and plagiarism begins is not difficult. Every well-taught student knows that it is never acceptable to take the exact sentences or paragraphs written by someone else and write them as if they are your own words. In most reputable institutions of higher learning (including most seminaries where pastors go to receive academic training), committing such an offense incurs severe penalties. Quotation marks and footnotes are important tools that should be properly used to help writers avoid intellectual theft.

For speakers, however, the line between research and plagiarism can sometimes be more easily blurred. If three sources agree on a syntactical point in a text, should the preacher cite any one or all of them? If an idea is sparked in your mind while listening to the sermon of another preacher must that fact be stated when expressing that idea in your own sermon? Can a preacher legitimately use the divisions of a biblical passage that he finds in a commentary? If so, should he cite the commentator?

All these, and many more, are legitimate questions that must be considered by every pastor who wants to rightly handle the Word of God in preaching.

Dr. David Schrock has given careful thought to this malady that plagues the modern church. In an age when both written sermons and audio recordings of preaching are readily available, the wisdom that he shares in this small book is priceless. With scholarly precision and pastoral care, David explains and demonstrates what faithful expositors are called to do and must avoid doing. He writes as a practitioner who is very familiar with the challenges of using the insights of others when speaking publicly. As such, this book is not so much a critique of pulpit plagiarism as it is a positive manual of how to avoid it. His labors have served both churches and those undershepherds whose responsibility it is to feed them week by week by serving them the Word of God.

This book should be in the hands of every seminary student and aspiring pastor to help direct them to careful habits that will serve them well in pursuing their calling. Those already in the regular rhythm of preaching will also benefit from the wisdom in this book, by using it as a guide to help maintain integrity in the main responsibility of their work.

All who love the Lord Jesus and are jealous for his glory to be manifested in the church through "the foolishness of preaching" are indebted to Dr. Schrock for this helpful tool.

Tom Ascol
Grace Baptist Church
Cape Coral, Florida
March 28, 2022

But thanks be to God, who in Christ always leads us in triumphal procession, and through us spreads the fragrance of the knowledge of him everywhere. For we are the aroma of Christ to God among those who are being saved and among those who are perishing, to one a fragrance from death to death, to the other a fragrance from life to life. Who is sufficient for these things? For we are not, like so many, peddlers of God's word, but as men of sincerity, as commissioned by God, in the sight of God we speak in Christ.

—2 Corinthians 2:14–17

Preface

A nyone who has ever listened to one of my sermons or read the title of this book might say it sounds a lot like John Piper. And you would not be far off. I do not make such a statement with conceit, daring to liken myself to one of the most influential preachers of my generation. Rather, I am simply acknowledging that aspiring pastors are bound to emulate solid, seasoned teachers.

Early in my twenties, I cut my teeth on Piper's sermons and books. For close to a decade I listened to his preaching regularly. So it is only natural that, when I began to preach, his speech patterns, style, and doctrinal emphases would affect my own.

Thinking back on his influence, I can still hear Piper's voice, with the sound of *seashells* resonating in my ears. And today, lines from one of his biographies or one of his *God-besotted* expositions often come to mind.[1] Indeed, Pastor John's teaching and writing have shaped my language, my theology, and my preaching immensely, as has the work of many other pastors, preachers, and teachers.

This is how all preachers are formed. No pastor is born in a vacuum, and each of us has tendencies drawn from those who have gone before him. Still, for all the ways Piper and others have influenced me, I have never preached one of their sermons. In college, when I began leading Bible studies, I used the notes of an older minister *one time*. Graciously, he offered them to me, and, for reasons of time and improvement (his notes were better than mine), I taught his material. Make that, I *tried* to teach his material.

Teaching the notes of someone else, in my experience, was a disaster. I didn't know the material—*his* material—and I fumbled all the way through it. Perhaps with more practice I could have mastered his material, but I vowed then and there, for good or bad, to always preach my own material, culled from my own study of the Word. By God's grace, for the last twenty years, I have kept that vow and always preached the Word of God with my own notes.

If this sounds boastful, it's not. It should not even be noteworthy. Every Lord's Day for the last two millennia, faithful servants of the Word have proclaimed the gospel from their personal study of the Word. They have labored over the text so that hungry souls would have living bread to eat. All of those brothers have had different abilities and different styles of delivery, but they have one thing in common—they preached God's Word according to their own honest, prayerful study. For generations this has been the way of the pastor.

Sadly, there are some today who do not seem to have that same conviction. Or, at least, they are more open to borrowing, sharing, or proclaiming ideas and words that are not original to them.

In the summer of 2021, this willingness to preach the sermons of others became a source of major contention in the Southern Baptist Convention. Just days after Ed Litton was elected convention president, it was revealed that he had repeatedly preached the sermons of J. D. Greear—the outgoing SBC president. Instead of calling for an inquiry or pushing pause on Litton's presidency, Greear threw his support behind Litton, even as the latter admitted to using Greear's sermons. Even more, Litton's church did the same.

Such a revelation caused great concern, and the internet exploded for weeks. But when it became apparent that nothing would be done, the clamor soon died down and the concern was forgotten. Only it wasn't.

Today, the topic of plagiarism in the pulpit continues to fill discussions on seminary campuses. While he has been supported by his friends, Ed Litton's name has become irrevocably connected to that topic. In short, the blemish caused by his practice of preaching other people's sermons has not been resolved. Worse, the unwillingness of his friends, his church, and his denomination to confront him not only shows a lack of love for him, but a disloyalty to the Word of God. Apparently, in our age of unapologetic pragmatism, peddling the Word of God is still fashionable (2 Cor. 2:17).

THE REASON FOR THIS BOOK

Going back to summer 2021, I wrote a number of blog posts on pastors and plagiarism.[2] Since then, I have continued to mull over this situation and what it means for plagiarism in the pulpit to be acceptable. If pastors are encouraged to use the work of others—with or without permission—I ask aloud: What effect will this have on the church, the pastoral office, and the preaching of God's truth? The church already suffers from a *credibility* problem, and if pastors are permitted to plagiarize, this problem will only be magnified.

So out of concern for the church, its pastors, and its people, I write this short book.

In the following pages, I will offer far more than a response to Ed Litton. I have nothing against him personally. If anything, I am concerned for the toll this imbroglio has taken upon his soul. This book is not an *ad hominem* attack on him. Instead, it is a salvo against the systemic practice of sharing and stealing sermons, a practice for which Litton is the most well-known recent example. The real genesis of this book is the collective "Meh!" and shrugged shoulders of Southern Baptists who have not taken sermon plagiarism more seriously. I will address concrete illustrations related to Ed Litton and matters in the Southern Baptist Convention, but the overall message is constructive, not carping.

With a desire to see churches built up, I offer this book as a short study of Scripture to see what God expects from his shepherds. After all, the job description of a pastor was not the brainchild of Lifeway, Vanderbloemen, or the Barna

Group. As the pastoral epistles tell us, pastors are called by God to bring the Word of God to the people of God. Therefore, the people of God and the men who teach and lead need to know—and abide by—what God expects of them.

Thus, in what follows, I will make a case that using the sermons of others is plagiarism, regardless of permission; that plagiarism never has a place in the church, let alone the pulpit; that every defense of the practice brings disrepute upon the church; and that churches should never shelter pastors who preach the work of others. Believe it or not, this book is far from an agitated rant. I will spend most of these pages outlining healthy habits for sermon formation and sermon annotation. Indeed, if Scripture itself is filled with citations and allusions to other texts, then it might have something to say about best practices for borrowing from others. How did the apostle Paul footnote? Inquiring pastors should want to know.

Thus, there is much for us to learn—or relearn—from Scripture on this subject. Too many churches and pastors have been enslaved by the gods of pragmatism, postmodernism, and packaging. Consequently, they have succumbed to treating pastors as performers instead of shepherds. What I am offering is an alternative vision for pulpit ministry. I am offering a biblical case for pastors to fulfill their primary calling by being pastor-teachers who equip the saints with a diet of biblical exposition.

To that end, I am riffing on, not ripping off, John Piper's *Brothers, We Are Not Professionals.*[3] In that book,

Piper doesn't touch on plagiarism, but he could have. In our day, a sustained argument against plagiarism in the pulpit is needed. It is needed because those pastors who have accepted the practice, or engaged in the practice, or endorsed the practice (even sharing their sermons), have forgotten what a pastor does and why preaching their own work is so important.

I will say it again: "Brothers, we are not plagiarists!" And by God's grace, may churches and their pastors repent of peddling the Word and recover a vision for true, biblical preaching.

Chapter 1

On Plagiarism and Preachers

WHY PLAGIARIZING SERMONS IS POPULAR BUT BIBLICALLY INDEFENSIBLE

It seems, frankly, utterly unthinkable to me that authentic preaching would be the echo of another person's encounter with God's Word rather than a trumpet blast of my own encounter with God's Word. Now to be sure, my sermon should be an echo. It should be an echo of the voice of God. But not an echo of an echo of the voice of God. So that is my conviction.

—John Piper [4]

W hen it comes to light that a pastor has been "echoing" the work of another—what we might euphemistically call sermon borrowing—it is deeply troubling. But it is even worse when that pastor has any influence on the life and ministry of other pastors because it says to younger men, who are finding their way in the wilderness of pulpit ministry, that it is acceptable to use the work of others.

To date, I can think of two pastors I knew personally who were fired for preaching someone else's sermons. I have heard many other reports of the same. [5] I can also think of ministries I have written off as unfaithful after learning that they were reheating the meals prepared by others. And last year, I watched the unbelieving world make sport of God's people because of plagiarism in the pulpit.[6]

Soon after the Southern Baptist Convention elected Ed Litton to be president, it came to light that he had, on numerous occasions, preached material from J.D. Greear. If you wonder what the extent of such "borrowing" is, you can watch his expositions of Romans 1 and Romans 8 online.[7] Both sermons demonstrate word-for-word dependence on Greear's work. In response, Greear and Litton released statements explaining the matter,[8] but with more than 140 sermons pulled from Litton's archive,[9] the trouble runs deeper.

Pastors and Plagiarism

Without getting into the specifics of the Litton situation, I want to step back and ask a few questions: Is it wrong for a pastor to borrow material from another? What does it mean to plagiarize in the pulpit? Why does this seem to be such a common practice? And what does Scripture say?

To start with, I am not the first to tackle this subject. Albert Mohler has discussed it, as have D.A. Carson, John Piper, and Andy Naselli with Justin Taylor.[10] Letting Carson speak for the whole, he expresses the severity of the problem.

> Taking over another sermon and preaching it as if it were yours is always and unequivocally wrong, and if you do it you should resign or be fired immediately. The wickedness is along at least three axes: (1) You

are stealing. (2) You are deceiving the people to whom you are preaching. (3) Perhaps worst, you are not devoting yourself to the study of the Bible to the end that God's truth captures you, molds you, makes you a man of God and equips you to speak for him.[11]

Carson's words are severe, and they are matched by the severity of others. Yet the consensus of these leaders does not mean there is an overall consensus. On the internet, you will find James Merritt offering permission to plagiarize his words,[12] websites selling sermon helps and pre-packaged sermon material,[13] and various sources encouraging pastors to partake in the practice of using the work that is not their own.[14] Thus, in what follows, we need to answer three questions:

1. What is plagiarism? Does it apply to borrowing the work of another when permission is received and attribution given?

2. Why is plagiarism so prevalent today? Who is championing it?

3. Is plagiarism biblically defensible? (My answer: No, it is not!)

By pursuing the answers to these questions, we can define our terms and evaluate from Scripture what God thinks about using the sermons of others.

WHAT IS PLAGIARISM?

Defining plagiarism should be relatively easy: It is using someone else's material without giving proper attribution.

Or, as Justin Taylor makes the point more finely, "'Plagiarism' involves using the original and specific wording or arguments of others without acknowledging the source, thus giving the impression that they are original with you."[15] Such a definition makes it clear that when a pastor uses the material of another *and does not give attribution,* he is plagiarizing.

If he does acknowledge the source in the message, then the problem moves from plagiarism to "sermon sourcing." This, too, is problematic, for reasons we will see in Scripture. But even before addressing the re-use of sermon material with permission and attribution, it is worth considering if such attribution escapes the charge of plagiarism.

In their helpful taxonomy of plagiarism, the good folks at Turnitin, an online resource for teachers spotting plagiarism, list ten types of plagiarism.[16] These ten types range from the copy-and-paste form of plagiarism to the "re-tweet"—an allusion to the practice of passing along someone's words on Twitter with the click of a button. In this taxonomy, they suggest that a re-tweet is a paper (or sermon) that "includes proper citation, but relies too closely on the text's original wording and/or structure."[17] In such an instance, the author acknowledges the source of the information, but he is still guilty of plagiarism because a single footnote in a paper is insufficient for properly citing the copious amount of information borrowed from the original source. The same applies to a sermon.

Understandably, this specificity makes the discussion about plagiarism more technical. But it also acknowledges the fact that even when permission and attribution are given, if the second sermon is a clone of the first, the issue of plagiarism remains.

The takeaway from re-tweet plagiarism is this: When we are talking about plagiarism in the pulpit, that label fits whether attribution is given to the original source or not. Whenever a pastor is making extensive use of someone else's work for his own sermon—with or without attribution— the term plagiarism still applies.

Now, one might object that Turnitin does not have a monopoly on defining plagiarism, and that we should explain the term with something more like Justin Taylor's definition. Maybe. But that only improves the matter slightly, and it may make it worse. If pastors are defending anything that comes close to plagiarism, the problem remains. By comparison, should the larger community of academics and communicators hold a higher standard than the church? Certainly not! If the world appears more honest than the heralds of truth, pastors have lost a hearing for the Truth before anyone gets to Sunday morning.

Wherever you land on the definition of plagiarism, I will use Turnitin's tenth type of plagiarism, the re-tweet, to address plagiarism in the pulpit. When pastors re-tweet other sermons, they are, to return to Carson's three points, (1) stealing, (2) deceiving others and (probably) themselves, and, most notably, (3) failing to live up to their calling as a pastor.[18]

Yet that calling may actually be the thing that divides Christians most on this subject. For those who define the pastor's calling according to the pastoral epistles seem to be at odds with those who define the pastor's calling in terms handed down from the modern professionalization of the pastorate. This difference may explain why so many have been defended the statements released by Greear and Litton, and why *Christianity Today* once offered a defense of plagiarism in the pulpit.

Why Is Plagiarism So Popular Today?

In 2002, *Christianity Today* offered a short editorial on the subject of plagiarism, called "When Pastors Plagiarize."[19] With a title like that, one might think that the editors would warn pastors against plagiarizing sermons. Yet *Christianity Today* did just the opposite.

Instead of explaining why pastors should preach their own work, they list three reasons why pastors plagiarize. In so doing, *Christianity Today* urged pastors to cite their sources and for churches to expect pastors to re-tweet the sermons of others. Here is their rationale:

1. **Pressure.** "We live in a media-saturated age in which we can watch, listen to, or read the brightest and best preachers at any time." Therefore, "the pressure on the local pastor to match this eloquence is felt on both sides of the pulpit."

2. **Comparison.** Because no other modern vocation is asked to generate as much content as the pastor who speaks multiple times a week, the pastor needs help in content creation. Politicians have a team of people

to help him or her, so it is natural for pastors to get help too.

3. **Isolation.** "The pastor is about the only public communicator today whose efforts are not collaborative or edited by others before they are made public." And any requirement that pastors must produce a sermon on their own is a "romantic illusion" that springs from the Enlightenment.[20]

For these reasons, the editors of *Christianity Today* make the case that pastors should freely use the work of others (while always giving credit to their sources) and that "congregations should allow, even encourage, their pastors to use the best material from books, magazines, and the Internet."[21]

With such an argument coming from such an influential magazine, it should not be surprising that pastors freely borrow the work of others. Ironically, the statements offered by Litton and Greear reflect *Christianity Today*'s argument and thereby prove that there is a stream of thought in the church today that stands against the strong denunciation of plagiarism in the pulpit.

This brings us back to the Bible with a bevy of questions: What does God think about such plagiarism? What does *he* expect of pastors, preaching, and plagiarism? If the Bible is our guide for all of life and godliness, then it must say something to us about pastors and the task of preaching. In their short editorial, *Christianity Today* simply assumes the modern context makes it permissible to re-tweet sermons, but is that what Scripture says? When it comes to plagiarism,

Christianity Today does not look to the Bible for answers, but we must.

What Does the Bible Say about Plagiarism?

Limiting our inquiry to the pastoral epistles (1–2 Timothy and Titus), we find five discreet truths about plagiarism and one general truth that speaks to the issue of the pastor and his vocation of handling the Word. Without giving a full exposition of any passage, we can discern a double-sided message from Paul: (1) Pastors show themselves approved before God and God's people by rightly handling God's Word in the study and the pulpit, and (2) pastors do not show themselves approved by peddling the Word and re-tweeting the works of others. With those two themes in mind, let's consider the wisdom given to Titus, Timothy, and all pastors everywhere.

1. Plagiarism Invites Teaching without Knowledge
(1 Timothy 1:3–7)

In 1 Timothy 1:3–7, Paul urges Timothy to remain in Ephesus and to contend with the false teachers arising in that city. Instead of teaching the truth of God's Word, which Paul calls a "stewardship from God," they "devote themselves to myths and endless genealogies, which promote speculation rather than . . . faith" (v. 4). Speaking of these false teachers, he writes, "Certain persons, by swerving from these, have wandered away into vain discussion, *desiring to be teachers of the law, without understanding* either what they are saying or the things about which they make confident assertions" (vv. 6–7, emphasis added).

The key point for our discussion of plagiarism is this: *Plagiarism invites teaching without understanding.* While some may argue that those who preach the work of others would only cite or re-tweet a sermon they understand, the truth is that we cannot understand *fully* what we borrow from others. Within the study of Scripture, there is a Spirit-led process of learning from God's Word that is essential for pastoral ministry and for faithful exposition.

In Paul's letter, he makes the point to Timothy that false teachers do not understand the law and how it brings people to the gospel of Jesus Christ (1:8–11). In our day, the rise of plagiarism also assures us that those speaking about the Word of God will have less personal knowledge of the truth they speak. This is John Piper's introductory point: Being an "echo of an echo," instead of exulting in the glories that you have personally seen in the Word of God, is an invitation for pastors to speak of what they do not know.

Again, the argument can be made that those who borrow material can learn from the brightest minds. But such knowledge is always second hand. As twentieth-century German theologian Helmut Thielicke observed in his book *A Little Exercise for Young Theologians*, "The man who is in the position of reproducing a lecture about Luther, or possibly giving one himself, perhaps knows nothing or almost nothing about all this, and can hardly know." Rather, this man "lives at second hand."[22]

In context, Thielicke is lamenting the "adolescent" seminarian whose knowledge about doctrine exceeds his knowledge of God. But the same problem applies here. If pastors are preaching the work of others, it will stunt their growth and hinder their own knowledge of God. As preaching professor Haddon Robinson has noted, expository preaching is the "communication of a biblical concept," derived from a rigorous study of the Bible, "which the Holy Spirit first applies to the personality and experience of the preacher, then through the preacher, applies to the hearers."[23] If preachers skip the study of God's Word for personal edification and rely on the work of others, they will endanger their own souls and the souls of their congregations.

To be clear, plagiarism doesn't produce unbelief, but it does promote a way of speaking that divorces biblical knowledge from existential knowledge. Because pastors already struggle to live up to the words they preach *when they do immerse themselves in studying God's Word,* the permission for and promotion of plagiarism will only produce a generation of pastors who teach without knowledge. And such teaching without knowledge can create a host of doctrinal and ethical problems.

2. Plagiarism Promotes Impersonal Communication (1 Timothy 1:12–17)

A few verses later in 1 Timothy, Paul details God's mercy in saving him and calling him to serve as an apostle (1:12–17). He describes his previous life as being "a blasphemer, persecutor, and insolent opponent" of Christ (v. 13), but because he received mercy, God has displayed in his very life what the gospel looks like. Indeed, Paul's testimony (repeated in Acts 9, 22, and 26) is given to the church to demonstrate what happens in conversion—the old man is put to death, and the new man is brought to life (cf. 2 Cor. 5:17).

Such is the nature of gospel ministry. A preacher speaks gospel truths as one recipient of grace inviting others to come and know the same. In such communications of the gospel, God uses vessels of mercy who have particular stories, gifts, and manners of speaking. No two preachers are the same. Yes, pastors will master the craft of preaching by listening to others, but to paraphrase D. A. Carson, if a preacher only listens to messages from one or two of his pastoral colleagues, he will sound like a cheap imitation. But if he listens to dozens of preachers, he will learn to develop his own voice.

One of the most important things a preacher can do is to grow comfortable in who God has made him to be and then to speak with the gifts God has given to him. I have pastored two churches, and my personality, education, and gifts served me well for one congregation, but not the other. Thankfully, I am now in a situation where my gifts match the church. But this fact needs to be recognized: A biblically qualified man will not fit in every congregation. And plagiarism inevitably leads to an ongoing impersonal ministry of the Word, even leading pastors to make use of illustrations and experiences that *others* have had.

Paul could proclaim the gospel through his personal testimony. Pastors who are true shepherds will do the same. As Peter tells elders to "shepherd the flock of God that is among you" (1 Pet. 5:2), so pastors should be preaching messages that arise from the life and strife of the congregations God has given them. When messages are borrowed from other locations, however, congregational specificity is endangered and preaching with a personal dimension is in jeopardy. Sure, attentive re-tweeters can supplement borrowed messages with personal stories, but that makes the message all the more artificial.

3. Plagiarism Threatens the Pastoral Office
(1 Timothy 3:1–7; cf. Titus 1:5–9)

When Paul turns to the qualifications of an overseer in 1 Timothy 3, he provides at least two reasons why plagiarism cannot work in the pulpit.

First, the overarching qualification for an elder is to be "above reproach." Both 1 Timothy 3 and Titus 1 list this qualification first, and Titus 1 lists it twice (vv. 5, 7). In the second occurrence, Paul says, "For an overseer, as God's steward, must be above reproach." Stewardship for Paul relates to teaching God's Word, and thus the one who brings God's Word must not have any moral or character flaws that would threaten the communication of that message.

But this is exactly what plagiarism does. Undetected plagiarism may not threaten the content of the gospel, but when it is discovered that the herald of the truth has not been truthful in citing his sources, all sorts of questions arise. When such knowledge is revealed, the watching world writes articles exposing the removal of past sermons and laughs at the church. And more harmful, others are less likely to listen to preaching of God's Word. After all, the world will say, "Pastors are charlatans, anyways." To avoid this kind of accusation, Paul says of the overseer, "He must be well thought of by outsiders, so that he may not fall into disgrace, into a snare of the devil" (1 Tim. 3:7).

When a pastor is not above reproach in his preaching, the unbelieving world is uninterested in *Christianity Today*'s defense of tired pastors borrowing sermons. Instead, they add plagiarism to their list of reasons for dismissing God's church and its life-giving message. If you haven't noticed, the reputation of pastors is not doing well today, and incidents of plagiarism, whether we think they are justified or not, do not help. God calls pastors to be above reproach so that we do not become a distraction to the truths of the gospel.

Second, elders are those who must be "able to teach" (1 Tim. 3:2; cf. Titus 1:9). Plagiarism undermines this pastoral qualification and makes it impossible to tell if someone is gifted to teach or if he is simply skilled to speak.[24] Worse, if a young preacher permits himself to use the work of others, he will never develop the gifts God has given him, which will lead to a perceived skill in preaching that does not match his actual gifting. To put it bluntly, plagiarism will inevitably misplace men in ministry.

For the sake of men called to preach and for the sake of their churches, we cannot permit pastors to re-tweet sermons. Such a practice is a recipe for long term disaster—for the preacher, for the local church, and for the universal church. Focusing on pastor themselves for a moment: One way men are sustained in ministry is by studying the Word, nourishing their own souls and bringing to their congregations the bread of life on which they have already fed. Plagiarism short-circuits this weekly rhythm, hindering the soul of the preacher, threatening the pastoral office, and changing the nature of gospel ministry.

4. Plagiarism Changes the Nature of Gospel Ministry (2 Timothy 2:1–2; James 3:1)

For those familiar with trends in ministry over the last century, you will not be surprised by the popularity of preachers borrowing sermon material or relying on teams for their sermon preparation.[25] As Gordon-Conwell professor David Wells has demonstrated time and again, pastors have become ministry managers, therapeutic counselors, and church-growth professionals.[26] This is a far cry from the biblical pattern of pastors as stewards of the Word and heralds of the truth. The current tendency to *encourage* borrowing sermon material, instead of repudiate it, is the sad but unsurprising fruit of losing a biblical approach to the pastorate.

When we go back to the pastoral epistles, however, we find something else entirely. We don't find teams collaborating to create sermons; we find gifted men who studied the Scripture and labored hard to feed the flock with the Word.

Most explicitly, Paul says in 2 Timothy 2:15, "Do your best to present yourself to God as one approved, a worker who has no need to be ashamed, rightly handling the word of truth." This verse, which addresses the individual preacher, single-handedly denies the place for borrowing material. Why? Because it is impossible to be approved as a faithful handler of God's Word if you are using someone else's best material.

Certainly, we could get into all the ways that pastors *rightly* lean on others in the process of sermon-writing.[27] It is true that every preacher depends on those who have gone before him. Commentaries and those who write them are gifts to the church. Any pastor who refuses to use them is fooling himself. Even Paul, in 2 Timothy 2:1–2, encourages Timothy to remember what Paul has said, so that he can teach faithful men who will then teach others. There is a place for preaching in community, but plagiarism sours the goodness of learning from others or preaching among a fraternity of preachers (as in Acts 13:1–3).

Because teachers will be judged more severely (James 3:1), they must give an account for what they teach and how they teach it. In the pastoral epistles, the elders who are gifted to teach are called to be stewards of the Word, faithful servants who teach sound doctrine from the Scriptures. Unfortunately, a culture of plagiarism changes the nature of this ministry. Pastors are led away from being prayerful disciples of God's Word to being skillful distributors of man's sermons. Such a change impairs the ability of the preacher to give an account for his words. And it denies the preacher the need to be skilled in biblical knowledge, languages, doctrine, or the wiles of the human heart. Freedom from doing the work of preparing sermons each week may open up times to do other ministry (counseling, discipling, etc.), but in the long run, the church is impoverished when its primary teacher is not steeped in the Bible.

In such instances, the pastor and his flock suffer from a deficiency of the Word. This may not be immediately evident, especially in a day when biblical literacy and theological depth are already lacking. Nevertheless, the bitter fruit will come. And when it comes, it may be too late for the shepherd and the sheep under his care.

5. Plagiarism Entices False Shepherds and Rewards Laziness (1 Timothy 6:5; 2 Timothy 2:1–7; 4:5)

In addition to the harm plagiarism does to the genuine pastor, allowing unoriginal teaching material also entices false shepherds to find a place in the church. Addressing the problem of false teachers, Paul warns Timothy of those who imagine that teaching God's Word is "a means of gain" (1 Timothy 6:5). Without assigning motives to those who have been exposed plagiarizing sermons, I submit that if a congregation permits borrowed material to be preached, it will only open the door to false teachers—either false in doctrine or false in desire.

Churches already have enough trouble calling pastors who will serve with good consciences, and pastors have enough trouble restraining their own ambitions for success in ministry. Adding the prospect of preaching slick sermons of someone else does nothing to mortify the pastor's desires for a larger congregation nor to protect the church from charlatans who are using the pulpit as a means of self-promotion. Just the opposite—it allures pastors to depend on the work of others. Thus, even if a church experiences a greater season of sermonic delivery following the use of re-tweeted sermons, in the long run, the costs will outweigh the benefits.

Closely associated with the desire for a larger church and the monetary gain that goes with it is the desire for greater ease. Preaching is hard work. And as with anything that is hard, the temptation to find shortcuts are many. Yet this temptation for ease is exactly where Paul speaks most directly: "As for you, always be sober-minded, endure suffering, do the work of an evangelist, fulfill your ministry" (2 Tim. 4:5) In short, Paul is saying to preachers of the Word, "Do the work!"

The bivocational pastor doesn't have to be the next Billy Graham or John Piper. The small-town pastor doesn't have to engage all the cultural challenges that Mark Dever does. Before the Lord and his heavenly court (2 Tim. 4:1), the faithful pastor must simply "preach the word; be ready in season and out of season; reprove, rebuke, and exhort, with complete patience and teaching" (v. 2). Nowhere in the pastoral epistles do we find a word about eloquence or erudition. It is all fidelity to the Scripture, but such fidelity means crucifying the desire to use the ministry as a means of gain and eschewing all temptation to laziness in preaching. By contrast, when plagiarism is embraced and encouraged, it does untold damage to the preacher and the church who receives his ministry. But even above the impact that can be seen is the impact that plagiarism has on the Word of God itself.

A FINAL WORD: PLAGIARISM DISHONORS THE WORD

The cumulative message of the pastoral epistles is to guard the flock by guarding sound doctrine. Preaching the Word is the work of the pastorate. There is nothing more important for a pastor than holding out God's Word to God's people every week. In that work, the pastor soon learns that what God has called him to is an impossible task. "Who is sufficient for these things?" (2 Cor. 2:16). Yet the faithful pastor, in prayerful dependence on the Lord, finds strength to do the work of the ministry in the power of the Spirit (cf. Col. 1:28–29).

Plagiarism destroys all of this. Not only does it turn preaching from a week-long communion with God and his Word to the rehearsed repetition of someone else's work, it also invites scrutiny and skepticism on the veracity of God's Word and the sincerity of God's gospel. Instead of protecting the Word and the flock, plagiarism endangers the flock and the right preaching of the Word. For this reason, pastors must spur each other on to fulfill their ministry of preaching the Word—a Word prepared during the week for the people they pastor.

Anything less than this fails to honor God's Word properly and invites disrepute on the Word of Life. For that reason above all others, as popular as plagiarizing sermons has become, it is biblically indefensible.

May God give us the courage of our convictions to stand against such practices. And may God strengthen his shepherds to continue to study the Word of God so that we would show ourselves approved as faithful shepherds of the flock that Christ purchased with his blood.

Chapter 2

The Sermon Begins in Your Study

WHY "APT TO TEACH" MEANS
MORE THAN "APT TO SPEAK"

For Ezra had set his heart to study the Law of the Lord, and to do it and to teach his statutes and rules in Israel.

—Ezra 7:10

Therefore an overseer must be above reproach, the husband of one wife, sober-minded, self-controlled, respectable, hospitable, able to teach . . .

—1 Timothy 3:2

In the summer of 2021, I sat in a room full of pastors talking about preaching, plagiarism, and what it means to be "apt to teach," a qualification given for elders in 1 Timothy 3:2 (KJV). I made the point that being "apt to teach" and "apt to speak" are not the same thing. And I said that because there seems to be great confusion about what it takes to be a pastor today. Should someone be a pastor just because he is a good communicator? Or should someone be a pastor because he is biblically qualified? And what do the biblical qualifications entail, anyways?

In some circles, being a good communicator seems to be the *sine qua non* of pastoral ministry. If someone can speak well, then he has what it takes to be a preacher. Never mind his weaknesses—if he can communicate in a way that connects, then he is a great cornerstone to building a vibrant church.

By contrast, Scripture gives a different and more complete picture. For instance, when defending his apostolic ministry, Paul testifies to his weakness in preaching. Referring to the super-apostles, whose speaking abilities may have exceeded his own, Paul notes, "For they say [of Paul], 'His letters are weighty and strong, but his bodily presence is weak, and his speech of no account'" (2 Cor. 10:10). Aware of his weaknesses, Paul defended his qualifications by appealing not to his charisma, but to his faithfulness to the truth and his suffering for that truth.

Today, such a perspective is under threat. Since the news broke concerning J.D. Greear and Ed Litton, I have heard anecdotal testimony from various pastors that many large church leaders see themselves as communicators of the truth more than shepherds of the flock or students of the Book. That's my way of phrasing it, and it certainly doesn't fit everyone. But with the popularity of groups like the Docent Research Group and Ministry Pass, as well as Lifeway's large selection of manuscripts free for the taking, it seems that one reason why so little concern has been raised by Ed Litton's use of J.D. Greear's sermons is that pastors preaching the work of others is something of an evangelical cottage industry.[28]

For me, I'm not interested in doing the investigative reporting on this subject, as some discernment blogs might. What I want to know is this: Is it *ever* appropriate for a pastor to preach someone else's sermon? Or, biblically speaking, is it a requisite pastoral qualification to preach what one has learned from his personal study of the Word? Faithful and enduring study of the Scripture, where the minister of the Word encounters the God of the Word, is my personal conviction, and it was the conviction of all of those pastors with whom I spoke last summer. But what does Scripture itself say? What does it mean to be "apt to teach"? Does teaching necessarily require the personal study of the Bible?

Thankfully, Scripture is not silent about these questions, and by returning to the pastoral epistles we can find solid answers.

APT TO TEACH MEANS MORE THAN APT TO SPEAK

To give my answer up front, I don't believe "apt to teach" means "apt to speak." Good speaking skills are not sufficient for a man to be pastor in a church, nor for a woman to preach to the congregation.[29] While it is true that effective teaching requires the ability to communicate well, more important than a pastor's speaking is the Word spoken and the man's qualifications to teach the congregation (see 1 Tim. 2:11–3:7; Titus 1:5–9). As the pastoral epistles make plain, the role of the pastor-teacher in the church has defined expectations. Those expectations focus on the character of the one preaching, but they also include (1) studying the word, (2) holding fast to the truth, and (3) showing progress before the congregation in how he handles the Word and himself.

Let's consider each of these three aspects of the pastor's vocation and how the ability to teach includes a willingness and dedication to study the Scriptures and to preach sermons that emerge from that study.

First, the office of the pastor is an office dedicated to studying the Scriptures.

In Acts 6, when administrative duties were increasing in Jerusalem and the Hellenistic widows were suffering as a result, the apostles took action to protect their role as servants of the Word. As Luke records, the leading apostles said to the fledgling church, "Therefore, brothers, pick out from among you seven men of good repute, full of the Spirit and of wisdom, whom we will appoint to this duty. But we will devote ourselves to prayer and to the ministry of the word" (vv. 3–4). Such should be the posture of every pastor. Above all, pastors are intercessors and expositors. Churches who long for the Word to prosper in their midst, as it did in Jerusalem, will make space for their pastors to study the Word and will expect them to do so.

Paul, too, sees the study of God's Word as a necessary duty of the pastor. In addition to defining pastors as teachers (Eph. 4:11) and calling Timothy to find reliable men who can teach others (2 Tim. 2:2), he says in 2 Timothy 2:15 that such men must be able to rightly handle the word of truth. A few verses later he addresses such men, saying that "the Lord's servant must . . . be able to teach" (2 Tim. 2:24). Previously, in 2 Timothy 2:1–7, he uses three illustrations that define the office of teacher: He must be single-minded like a soldier (v. 4), honest in competition like an athlete (v. 5), and hard-working like a farmer (v. 6).[30] Put these together and you have the picture of a pastor as a soldier who doesn't find a proxy for his service, a pastor as an athlete who doesn't deceive his Judge (or the Judge's children), and a pastor as a farmer who works hard in sowing and reaping (cf. 1 Cor. 3:6–9). And what is the seed that the farmer uses? It is the Word of God that he has beheld in his study (see e.g., Luke 8:11). Whether he is studying the works of God in his office (see Ps. 111:2) or reading parchments in prison (see 2 Tim. 4:13), the faithful pastor is a slave to Scripture. This is how Paul identified himself, and it is how churches identify pastors today.

To boil it down to basics, the pastoral office as Paul defines it is a studious office. As Covenant Theological Seminary professor Robert Yarbrough comments on 1 Timothy 3:2,

> it is self-evident that a movement founded by a consummate teacher, whose followers were tasked with spreading his legacy by teaching others what he had taught them (Matt 28:18–20), would need skilled teachers at the helm. Paul had been teaching at least since Barnabas had discovered him and brought him to Antioch (Acts 11:25–26), if not indeed from the very time of his conversion (Acts 9:20). Timothy was expected to do likewise (2 Tim 2:2).[31]

Clearly, teaching stands at the center of the church's mission, just as it did in Jesus's Great Commission. Jesus commanded his disciples "to make disciples of all nations . . . *teaching* them to obey all that I have commanded you" (Matt. 28:19, emphasis added). As it has been often noted, disciples are not mere converts; they are apprentices who give themselves to their master's teaching (cf. Matt. 13:52). That's the explicit teaching of Jesus, and the underlying assumption is that teaching requires study. We know this by Jesus's own life and the background of the Old Testament.

As evidenced by his discussion with scribes in the temple (Luke 2:46) and his use of the Old Testament in his teaching, Jesus grew up studying the Scriptures. He also expected his audiences to know the Scriptures ("Have you not read . . . ?" in Matt. 12:3, 5; 19:4; 22:31; etc.). Similarly, the disciples' knowledge of the Law came by their learning from Jesus (Acts 4:13). All of this stands on the shoulders of Israel's prophetic tradition, which made studying the Word of God the baseline for all faithful teaching (cf. Lev. 10:11; Ezra 7:10). For all these reasons and more, the pastoral office is a studious vocation. And those who cannot, or will not, study the Scriptures *for themselves* should not stand in the congregation proclaiming the Word, nor hold the office of pastor.

Second, elders are created and maintained by holding fast to God's Word.

A number of years ago I preached a sermon on Titus 1:9, answering this question: Where do elders come from? And my answer was that elders are created by holding fast to the

Word of God. As that verse declares, "[The overseer] must hold firm to the trustworthy word as taught, so that he may be able to give instruction in sound doctrine and also to rebuke those who contradict it."[32] In sum, the overseer must be able to teach truth and to refute error. But such an ability to declare and defend the faith means he has studied the Word.

Encouragingly, this means that erudition, economic class, and eloquence are *not* requirements for pastors. Seminary may be helpful, but Scripture does not require pastors to have letters after their names. Jesus found his disciples in the fishing boats of Galilee, not in the schools of Jerusalem. This teaches us that schooling is not the requirement, but adherence to God's Word is. In that sermon, I made the point that the key qualification for an elder and his teaching is that this man must "hold fast" to God's Word such that it reforms his life and renews his mind.

Actually, in Paul's letters, this idea of holding fast abounds. In 1 Timothy 1:19, we find that those "holding faith" (clinging to the truth) can serve the Lord and his church. Conversely, when men let go of God's Word, they will shipwreck their faith (vv. 19–20). Could it be that many prominent pastors have ran their ministries aground because they have failed to hold fast to the personal study of Scripture? I can't speak definitively, but the connection seems more than plausible. And if we now find a string of pastors borrowing the work of others, it won't be long before some of them are unstrung. I do not say this with any sense of glee—only urgency!

Back to Paul and the need to hold fast to the Word. Pastors must be able to know the difference between myths and truth (1 Tim. 4:7), and they can only do that as they train themselves for godliness (v. 8; cf. Heb. 5:11–14).[33] A few verses later, Paul encourages Timothy to "immerse" himself in the Word (1 Tim. 4:15). And, finally, in 1 Timothy 6:11–12, 20–21, Paul uses words like "pursue," "fight," "take hold," and "guard" to stress the importance of the work and the strength needed to endure. In short, elders must hold fast to the Word like a man clings to a life preserver in a raging sea. As Jonathan Edwards put it, the only way an elder can do that is "to study the Scriptures so steadily, constantly, and frequently" that he may find himself growing "in the knowledge of the same."[34]

Woe to the pastor who studies the Scriptures to get his union card for ministry (i.e., a seminary degree) and then adopts the habit of letting others study the Scriptures for him. A faithful husband wouldn't let another man study his wife so that the busy husband can give her a love letter with the adorations of a cuckold. Neither will a true shepherd permit another man to do the work of studying the Scripture for the sheep he is called to pastor. This doesn't mean we don't learn from others, quote others, or depend on others. But it does mean that there is a genuine communion with God in the study that translates to the pulpit.

Third, pastors should have such a close relationship with their congregations that the flock can see the progress of their shepherd in both doctrine and life.

This last point is a bit wordy, but it comes directly from the mind of Paul and his admonition to Timothy. In 1 Timothy 4:11–16, the apostle calls Timothy to uphold the Scriptures and to model the faith before the eyes of the church in Ephesus. He writes,

> Command and teach these things. Let no one despise you for your youth, but set the believers an example in speech, in conduct, in love, in faith, in purity. Until I come, devote yourself to the public reading of Scripture, to exhortation, to teaching. Do not neglect the gift you have, which was given you by prophecy when the council of elders laid their hands on you. *Practice these things, immerse yourself in them, so that all may see your progress.* Keep a close watch on yourself and on the teaching. Persist in this, for by so doing you will save both yourself and your hearers. (emphasis added)

In this imperative-rich paragraph, Paul orients Timothy to the ministry of the Word that should shape his life and his calling. In particular, his instructions create a tight relationship between Timothy the pastor (or apostolic delegate) and the congregation. Indeed, while too many pastors have experienced an adversarial relationship with their churches, the biblical ideal is one of fellowship and shared communion in Christ and his Word. As a result, pastors are not preparing a Bible lesson for people they don't know; they are preaching God's Word to a people they do know. Such personal knowledge can never be provided by Docent, Ministry Pass, or any other research group. It can only come from a pastor who knows his people.[35]

For now, we can clearly see that Paul calls Timothy to serve as a personal model for a particular people. In other words, the church at Ephesus must really know Timothy, what his life is like, and how his ministry of the Word does or does not affect him. Simultaneously, the church should be able to observe that this man of God is "progressing" in his handling of the Word (v. 15). As I have heard multiple times from David Helm, a pastor at Christ Church Chicago, in his preaching seminars, "Your people need to see your *progress*." But this assumes that the pastor is actually doing the work of studying the Scripture—for his life, his doctrine, and his regular ministry of preaching.

While Paul's letters are directed to the work of the minister, these same letters offer insight for churches. Shepherds are assigned to local churches, and local churches are responsible for knowing and evaluating the life and ministry of their shepherds. Why else would Paul give his lists of elder qualifications in 1 Timothy 3 and Titus?

Practically, the best way to see fruit in an overseer is not through a yearly evaluation, but in a life that is immersed in the Word and that is leading others to make progress in God's Word. Such progress can only happen as a pastor gives himself to a local congregation and a local church fulfills their calling of supporting and submitting to *qualified* elders. When that occurs, the church grows in the Word of God with the man of God—or, better, the men of God who make up a plurality of elders. But when the relationship between pastor(s) and people is not upheld, the communication of the Word simply becomes an impersonal download of biblical information—figuratively and literally.

I realize that many churches are designed for such impersonal communicators of the gospel, that congregants have grown accustomed to *not* knowing their pastors, and that mega-churches are enticed to promote men who are gifted communicators. But as we have already discovered, apt to teach does not mean the same thing as apt to speak. Rather, being apt to teach means that someone is gifted as a teacher, but such gifting includes a desire and ability to study the Word of God before he communicates it. Similarly, in context, being apt to teach means a desire to teach a people with whom he is sharing his life, not just his notes (see 1 Tim. 2:8).

Such a commitment to biblical study and personal knowledge is being lost today. But that doesn't mean reformation cannot come. It just means there is a need for repentance. That repentance begins with those who have made a habit of preaching the work of other men, but it also means churches must repent for permitting such practices to go on.

God's Providence in the Plagiarism

Perhaps the debacle of speakers using the words of other speakers will spur God's people—his shepherds and his sheep—to get back to the basics of biblical ministry. I am hopeful that, in God's providence, the exposure of plagiarism in the Southern Baptist Convention will serve as a warning to all of us. May it put a bitter taste in our mouth for taking the sugar-stick sermons of others and preaching them as our own. Clearly, God intends for his pastors to do the work of the ministry, which begins in the study and continues into a personal knowledge of the flock.

Apt to teach is not the same thing as apt to speak. By God's grace, may our Christ, the Great Shepherd of the sheep, grant the church a fraternity of teachers who faithfully study the Word and preach that Word to the people they know and love.

Chapter 3

"But He Just Gets Me"

Three Responses to Pragmatic Arguments for Plagiarism

S uppose there was a church where the pastor was disqualified from ministry because of verbal and physical abuse toward his congregation or family. He preached each Sunday while holding his Bible in hands marked by violence, and, in his unrepentance, even divorced his wife. But what if you talked to a man or woman from that church who lamented the pastor's exit by saying something like, "I know he had his problems, but his sermons always spoke to me. He just gets me."

In such an instance, personal sentiments have far eclipsed biblical standards. Ignoring whether this man was objectively qualified to preach, his listener's subjective interest was in having someone who made him or her feel a certain way. Such is the case in many churches today.

Rather than upholding pastors to the biblical standards of leadership, many churchgoers are looking for someone with a certain gift of charisma, inspiration, or entertainment. These days, it seems that Ted (as in TED Talks) has replaced

Timothy and Titus as the standard for good preaching. And communication skills have exceeded the importance of godly character.

To that point, I once talked with an elder from a large church who argued for their multi-campus model on the basis of the senior pastor's extraordinary giftedness in preaching. More specifically, he said that if this man didn't preach, people would leave the church. So instead of trying to utilize different campus pastors, they recorded the senior pastor's sermons and replayed them at the various locations. This is pragmatism at its finest.

Addressing the Pragmatism of Pulpit Plagiarism

In this chapter, I'm not going to address the problems of multi-site churches or what makes for good preaching. Instead, I want to address the pragmatism that funds those churches and invites churchgoers to value charisma over character. More specifically, I want to address the way pragmatism leads to and results from a defense of plagiarism in the pulpit.

In chapters 1 and 2, I've argued, respectively, that sermon plagiarism is biblically indefensible and that the biblical model for preachers is that of the gifted *teacher*, not a gifted *speaker*. Now, however, I want to respond to three pragmatic arguments that were raised when chapter 1 was still a blog post. To cite the argument in full, I will share what one commenter said. Questioning my charge against Ed Litton's plagiarism in the pulpit, he or she responded:

We've had this issue brought up in our church recently. I personally don't feel as strongly against using another's sermon or outlines because it can and will still be used by the Holy Spirit to save lost souls and minister to the hurting. The author seems to me to assume that God doesn't have the power to use sermons, regardless of who wrote them, to be impactful and may that they may even be harmful....?! [sic] That "logic" makes little sense. The biggest issue I would have would be if a pastor claimed the upcoming series or that day's message as something he had written himself, slaved over all week, etc.

I am on the Worship Team at church. I, we, feel gifted with voice and called to use that gift to reach others week after week. However, we don't acknowledge the Spirit filled lyric's writers, the composers of those songs or hymns every week! No[t] once. And yet ... hearts are touched, tears of joy flow and lives can be impacted by a song of worship and praise. Preaching a sermon written by another man of God doesn't mean it's any less impactful or blessed! I have witnessed this myself. [I heard] a message preached that was written by another pastor. And souls were saved, congregants fell at the altar to repent, lives were truly touched that day and in the last few months after. How can that be bad?! Satan is, for sure, not the one seeing to it souls are saved! That's God Almighty!

> I truly feel it's a large sect of pastors who say/think, "Well, I put in the study time and doggone it, so should they!" And while I sort of get that, you are all on the same team. . . . God's Team, the Lord's Army! This division is destructive and unhelpful.

Often, blog comments offer darkened counsel. At other times, however, a comment can be illuminating, because it says out loud what others are thinking about the subject in question. In this case, the comment provides a counterargument to mine. And for that I am thankful. In what follows, I will attempt to respond to the stated objections.

To begin, it is certainly true that plagiarism in the pulpit, combined with a general defense of the practice, is divisive—and, by extension, Satanic. But I do not believe the division comes from calling out the practice. Just the reverse, the problem stems from pastors and churches peddling the Word and permitting pastors to preach re-tweeted sermons.

As I have tried to make clear, qualified pastors must be men formed by the Word, in order to feed the flock with the Bread of Life by bringing God's food from the text to the table. In other words, just as God told Adam that he would make bread by the sweat of his brow, so pastors must do the same. We do not bring grain to the flock of God, but fully prepared bread. And we do not deliver what someone else has prepared, even if the thorns of study make such microwave meals attractive. Rather, servants of the Word are the preparers of the meal—presenting the Bread of Life from the Words of Life, enabled by the Spirit of Life.

Still, not supposing that such a vision of pastoral ministry is naturally accepted today and hearing too many instances of churchgoers wanting a preacher who "gets them," I want to answer three pragmatic arguments that are used to defend pastors who use the material of others.

THREE RESPONSES TO PRAGMATIC ARGUMENTS FOR PLAGIARISM

1. Pastors are shepherds and teachers, not performers.

To go over ground I covered before, pastors must be defined by the word of God, not the preferences of modern churchgoers. David Wells has been most emphatic on this point, as he has shown how the role of pastor has moved from the realm of teaching biblical theology to providing therapeutic counsel.[36] In other instances, business models replace biblical models; the pastor is likened to a CEO instead of a shepherd.

While some may not appreciate the significance of such metaphors, to frame the pastor as a business leader or therapeutic sage is to change his role. Similarly, to liken the pastor to a musician who sings the songs of another is to confuse his vocation. Here is how the aforementioned commenter makes the point:

> I am on the Worship Team at church. I, we, feel gifted with voice and called to use that gift to reach others week after week. However, we don't acknowledge the Spirit filled lyric's writers, the composers of

> those songs or hymns every week! No[t] once. And
> yet . . . hearts are touched, tears of joy flow and lives
> can be impacted by a song of worship and praise.
> Preaching a sermon written by another man of God
> doesn't mean it's any less impactful or blessed!

I agree with this argument, as far as it goes. But where it goes too far is to apply the standards of a musician to the standards of a pastor.[37] For starters, there are not biblical qualifications for singers or musicians in the New Testament. If there are worship leaders in the New Testament, then the plurality of elders should fill that role. In the Old Testament, the musicians and singers were the Levites, who were set apart for service in the temple (see 1 Chronicles 22–26).

Rightly understood, pastors are the ones who lead the church in congregational worship, and thus the same biblical qualifications should apply to ones leading the church in song. Now, in most cases, those singing/playing are not upheld to the qualifications of a pastor. And I am not arguing they should be. But I am making the point that to compare a pastor feeding his flock with the sermons of Tim Keller or Matt Chandler to a musician singing the songs of Isaac Watts or Chris Tomlin is a category mistake.

The closer comparison is between musicians and Sunday School teachers. I would not cry foul if a children's teacher used *The Gospel Project* for their Sunday School lesson, even if they read the whole thing from the book. Most Sunday School teachers are not elders, or elder-qualified. And the expectation of such teachers is not that they would prepare their own materials. That might be aspirational for some teachers, but not a uniform expectation.

The same caveat applies to situations where Christians are present, but preachers are not. Throughout church history, printed sermons have been read privately and corporately with great effect. In such a case where a qualified elder is absent, reading the text of a sermon is commendable.[38] But it is commendable, in part, because everyone knows that the man reading the sermon is *reading someone else's sermon.*

For pastors who are leading their flocks, however, it is different. Pastors are not performers who play the chords that others compose; they are not Sunday School teachers who use the provided curriculum. Instead, they are both expected and employed (in the case of vocational elders) to study the Scriptures and teach the people from their own personal labors (1 Tim. 5:17–18). When they simply recite the material of others, however, they are demonstrating that they are not qualified to be pastors. They might make reliable Sunday School teachers, but they are not gifted to teach a whole congregation from God's Word. Why? Because pastors are teachers, not performers.

2. Apparent fruit doesn't justify immoral practices.

When Jonathan Edwards witnessed the First Great Awakening, he offered a careful evaluation of true and false fruit in his work *Religious Affections.*[39] In that volume, he remarked that one of the great signs of true salvation is the enduring effect of holiness, love, and humility in the life of Christian.

By contrast, intense emotions, physical sensations, and immediate signs of the Spirit, subjectively perceived, do not guarantee the actual work of the Spirit.

With the rise of revivalism that came in the Second Great Awakening and the experience-oriented approach to ministry that followed, Edwards' biblical and theological understanding of conversion was effectively lost. Today, it is not holiness by which a ministry is measured; instead it is happiness, healing, or the ability to manufacture an emotional high. Accordingly, the measure of a preacher's effectiveness is not tested by his character or the enduring fruit of his ministry; it is measured by the way people feel in and after a service.

Because of this commitment to pragmatism, it doesn't matter if the preacher has labored in his study to bring a message to the people or if he is using someone else's material. To those who are at church to have a good time or feel the Spirit, it matters little if the performer is a cover band instead of the genuine article. *Experience* is the thing. As our commenter noted,

"Preaching a sermon written by another man of God doesn't mean it's any less impactful or blessed! I have witnessed this myself. [I heard] a message preached that was written by another pastor. And souls were saved, congregants fell at the altar to repent, lives were truly touched that day and in the last few months after. How can that be bad?!"

Yes, how can it be bad?

That question is worth considering. And *Christianity Today's* exposé on Mars Hill helps answer the question.[40] In this serial podcast, Mike Cosper tells the history of the church that rose and fell around the ministry of Mark Driscoll. In the series trailer, one of the pragmatic arguments for letting Driscoll's giftedness outrun his godliness went like this: "The prevailing justification for pretty much all the carnage that happened within Mars Hill was, 'Hey, look at the fruit.'" This sentiment is pure, undiluted pragmatism. And it applies to sermon plagiarism just as it does to church growth.

Indeed, until they collapsed, Mark Driscoll's preaching ministry and Mars Hill's church-planting model were judged to be wildly successful because of their numeric results. But counting numbers to justify a ministry demonstrates a commitment to success, not Christ. While size is the measure of success in America, the Bible has a different metric. And that metric relates to Christlikeness and spiritual fruit—not to the ever-increasing expansion of bodies, budgets, and buildings. Sadly, too many Christians confuse these.

Returning to Scripture, the pastoral qualifications are always measurements of holiness, as given by the Spirit of holiness. Only men whose lives are marked by the Spirit and his gift of teaching should stand before the congregation and proclaim God's Word. Mars Hill is not the only church that has blown up—in both senses of the word—because of pragmatism. Often, pragmatic methods of ministry do work, but only for a season. And this is the problem with preaching the sermons of another.

While such sermons may draw a crowd or build a church, the practice is not good for the soul of the preacher. Nor is it good for the health of the church. Even more, as it becomes known that a pastor is using the work of others, the reputation of the church will be compromised and the truth of the gospel will be questioned.

So how bad is it when "fruit" is born with bad seed? It's really bad, because it provides cover for immoral practices in the pulpit—namely, stealing, lying, and coveting.

3. The Spirit of holiness cannot bless lawbreaking.

In the Ten Commandments, the final three are these (Exod. 20:15–17):

> You shall not steal.
>
> You shall not bear false witness against your neighbor.
>
> You shall not covet your neighbor's [sermon] or . . . anything that is your neighbor's.

Okay, "sermon" is not in the original, but sermons would fit under the category of "anything that is your neighbors." Written by Spirit-led men who study the Scriptures, sermons are gifts that pastors give to their congregations. In this way, a sermon should not be understood as "his own." Possessiveness is never a healthy habit for pastors.

That being said, a sermon *is* the intellectual property of the preacher, and it should be treated as such.[41] Thus, to preach someone else's sermon breaks either the eighth, ninth, or tenth commandments, if not all of them. To see this more clearly, let's consider each in order.

First, any time someone uses the work of another without his permission, it is stealing. This is true whether the first person appears to have lost intellectual property or not.[42] Stealing is not excused just because someone claims that the owner was not deprived of the item in question. Nor is sermon stealing excused by some appeal to Philippians 1:17–18:

> The former proclaim Christ out of selfish ambition, not sincerely but thinking to afflict me in my imprisonment. What then? Only that in every way, whether in pretense or in truth, Christ is proclaimed, and in that I rejoice.

Under God's gracious providence, truth preached with bad motives can have a good effect. But let's not pretend that stolen sermons taste sweet to God. Judges 17:1–6 teaches us that when a thief deserves a curse but receives a blessing instead, God's judgment has come upon his people because they have fallen into moral chaos. Such is our current condition. Pastors and their people are defending the practice of taking sermons. This is not good.

Second, if a pastor receives permission to preach another's work but fails to give attribution, it may not be stealing (technically), but it is bearing false witness. When an agreement is made—with or without monetary payment—between two pastors to share their material and either congregation is in the dark, a false witness has been born. Lest we think this is a small thing, consider the fact that the New York Times ran an article reporting on just such a story, calling it "Sermongate."[43] Again, the unbelieving world may be more honest about this matter than pastors who are swapping sermons.

Finally, preaching the work of another suggests that coveting stands somewhere behind the controversy. Without attempting to discern motives, the act of using another's sermon raises the question: Why is it so inviting to preach another man's sermon? I wouldn't Photoshop a picture of another man's church and call it my own, so why would I preach his sermon? A video promotion by Ministry Pass a few years ago suggests that one answer is *busyness*.[44]

Because of busyness, Ministry Pass suggests that a pastor may need help to stay at the top of his game. And so, the argument goes, it is perfectly acceptable to rely on the work of others. Unfortunately, such busyness may be a symptom of another problem: laziness. As Eugene Peterson has stated, a busy pastor is a lazy pastor. Here is his rationale:

> *I am busy because I am lazy.* I indolently let others decide what I will do instead of resolutely deciding myself. I let people who do not understand the work of the pastor write the agenda for my day's work because I am too slipshod to write it myself. The pastor is a shadow figure in these people's minds, a marginal person vaguely connected with matters of God and good will. Anything remotely religious or somehow well-intentioned can be properly assigned to the pastor.[45]

Do you see what he is saying? Pastors are busy because they are too lazy to lead the people God has entrusted to them *in the way God has commanded them*. Instead, to please people or to make themselves look good, pastors do everything in the ministry—everything other than the most important thing. And what is the most important thing? It is feeding the flock with the Word of God and prayer!

As I observed in chapter 2, pastors-as-speakers have already lost track of what a pastor is supposed to be. So it would not be surprising that, in the whirlwind of doing dozens of things that pastors were never intended to do, they justify the need to borrow the work of others to do the one thing God has called them to do—preach faithful sermons. Sadly, this is a pressure that is exacerbated by a performance-driven mentality, and it is a pressure that many pastors accept as a necessary evil.

This necessary evil is perpetuated not only because more than a few men have made the practice common, but also because men look at the impressive ministries of others and think, *That's what I want.* Such a desire for a flourishing ministry is not inherently sinful, but it is a temptation that has led many to idolatrous practices in ministry. And remember, Paul likens covetousness to idolatry (Col. 3:5).

Tragically, this kind of thinking is akin to the man who pursues pornography (or adultery) out of a spirit of covetousness. Remember, the tenth commandment specifically calls men to not covet another's wife. Instead, when a married man sees a beautiful woman who is not his wife, it should spur him on to tend his own garden and love his own wife. Read Proverbs 5. It is unhealthy and unnecessary for a man to deny a woman's beauty (cf. Gen. 29:17), but it is abominable for him to covet her for himself. Instead, beauty in general should lead him to delight in the beauty of his own wife.

By analogy, when a pastor hears beauty in the well-formed words of another, he should be spurred on to love God, study God's Word, and preach excellent sermons for his church.[46] If he wants to preach and doesn't have a church, he should never seek a church by preaching the sermons of others. He should seek the Lord and "fan into flame" the gifts God has given him (cf. 2 Tim. 1:6). Becoming a preacher takes time, and every good preacher will be shaped by others, but to become the mouthpiece of another man—instead of God—is to invalidate the preacher's ministry.

Whatever motivation leads to preaching another pastor's work, there is a heart issue involved somewhere. This heart issue may be related to the eighth and ninth command-ments—do not steal and do not lie—but it is also related to the tenth—do not covet. Rightly understood, the Ten Commandments do not just deal with external actions, they address the heart. And when a man sees that another man's sermon is "a delight to the eyes," "good for food," and that it will "make one wise" before others, such a man is being led astray on the same path that took down Adam and Eve (cf. Gen. 3:6). This is how serious preaching someone else's sermon is. It is not simply a matter of best practices in preaching, but it stands at the heart of the gospel ministry and the ongoing testimony of the church and her preachers.

Still, such an opinion is not shared by everyone. Again, as my blog commenter framed it:

> I personally don't feel as strongly against using another's sermon or outlines because it can and will still be used by the Holy Spirit to save lost souls and minister to the hurting. The author seems to me to assume that God doesn't have the power to use sermons, regardless of who wrote them, to be impactful and may that they may even be harmful....?! [sic] That "logic" makes little sense.

Here is the question: Can the Holy Spirit, i.e., the Spirit of truth and holiness, "use" a sermon that breaks the eighth, ninth, or tenth commandments? Sure. God can "use" anything to accomplish his purposes. Just consider how he preached truth through the mouth of a donkey—and here I refer to Balaam, not his beast of burden (see Numbers 22–24). God can bring good from the evil actions of men— look at Joseph and his brothers (Gen. 50:20). God can even ordain the breaking of his law in order to fulfill his law— this is what Peter says of the cross in Acts 2:23. Yet *using* a sermon is not the same thing as *blessing* a sermon. God does not bless those who serve him with immoral means, and ministries built with such wood, hay, and stubble will, in time, be proven fruitless.

Again, large numbers, big churches, and high emotions do not ultimately prove a man's ministry. Nor should they protect him when questions of stealing, deceiving, and using others' sermons surface. Truly, the pragmatic argument that God can use any man's sermon as long as it has some modicum of truth is not sufficient for allowing pastors to preach work that is not their own. If this is not obvious for the biblical reasons cited above, may the Lord have mercy. Perhaps, in that mercy, he is beginning to expose these faulty practices so that others would be warned.

Returning to God's Standards for Pastors and Preaching

To revisit an argument I made earlier, if a pastor must depend upon preaching the work of another, that man should not a teaching pastor. Clearly, such a man is not gifted to teach, even if he is undeniably able to speak. The gift Christ gave to the church was a battery of Spirit-filled pastor-teachers (Eph. 4:11). Shepherds who feed the flock with God's Word are God's plan. And despite the many ways churches confuse the office of pastor and contort the contents of his job description, the Word of God remains true.

Truly, if we let the inspired wisdom of the Bible speak to the corrupting pragmatism of our day, then churches should be asking why they are supporting someone who is simply copy-and-pasting the work of others. Such a sermon thief should not be holding the office of pastor or holding out the Word of Truth. Just as importantly, churches should not be exalting or excusing such an imposter. They should, instead, be looking to the standards of the pastoral office to evaluate the work their pastor is or is not doing.

In this way, churches should expect that their pastor (or pastors) is one who is laboring in the Word to preach and teach. Similarly, if a pastor has a church that has so shackled him with other non-pastoral responsibilities—i.e., changing the church sign, cleaning the building, printing the bulletins, etc.—he should be calling others to join him so that he can equip the saints for their works of ministry (Eph. 4:12). This is what pastor-teachers do. When they fulfill their calling, the church will grow in health. But when they do not do the work of studying and teaching, the church will not grow in health, regardless of how much it grows in size.

For this reason, it is vital that we abandon the pragmatic arguments for plagiarism in the pulpit. All of us—pastors and congregations alike—must return to the biblical model of shepherd-teachers who feed the flock with God's Word. For, in fact, it doesn't matter whether a pastor "gets you." What we all need to "get" is Christ, and Christ will only be found when his church is ordered according to his revealed word. It was for that reason that Paul wrote his pastoral epistles—to make sure that the churches under his watch stayed true to their calling as "a pillar and buttress of the truth" (1 Tim. 3:15; Titus 1:5). For those of us today who defend sermon swapping and plagiarism in the pulpit, we need to repent and return to the way God ordered his church.

May God help us rediscover the biblical standards for pastors and preaching.

Chapter 4

A Fraternity of Qualified Elders

SERMON TEAMS ACCORDING TO THE BIBLE

In the wake of Ed Litton's admission of using the sermons of other preachers, there came another revelation that his sermons were developed with a team of eight members from his church. In his statement regarding the use of J.D. Greear's sermons, Litton wrote,

> We employ a preaching team approach at Redemption Church that is comprised of eight men from our staff/congregation who meet weekly to discuss study insights, outlines, and approaches to the text. This sermon prep process includes working in the languages, consulting commentaries and books, and listening to strong communicators. In that process, I learned about my friend J.D. Greear's messages on Romans and discovered what he had recently preached resonated with the direction God was leading me and our preaching team. We often consulted his manuscripts along with other resources as we prepared.[47]

Here we find an unapologetic defense for a team approach to preaching. This leads to questions about what a sermon team does or does not do. In the wake of a plagiarism scandal, it is only appropriate to ask such questions. To put it cynically, does a sermon team do the work of studying Scripture for the pastor? Or ambivalently, does the sermon team simply assist the pastor with his study—maybe all the time or just when the pastor is returning from vacation? Or positively, is the sermon team a way in which a pastor is developing a team of current and future pastors? What is going on and who is influencing whom is vitally important for discerning the appropriateness or inappropriateness of such a collaboration.

If sermon teams are strategically designed to prepare men for future service in the church, there is every reason to support them. Every healthy church should be recognizing, equipping, and calling gifted teachers. Alternatively, if a sermon team is created to assist the lead pastor so that his on-stage performance reflects the labors of others, then other questions arise. How much does the pastor depend upon the insights, observations, and language of his team? Is it every Sunday, or just once in a while? Does the solid theology (or woke ethics) of the preacher come from his own convictions, or from a team of ghostwriters? Even more, how much does he need to give credit to his sermon team for powerful illustrations and textual explanations? And what about faults? Who is to blame if the pastor errs? In the aforementioned statement, Litton's culpability is spread to his entire team. Yet when Paul brings his measuring rod to the ministry, he has individuals in mind.

> According to the grace of God given to me, like a skilled master builder I laid a foundation, and someone else is building upon it. Let each one take care how he builds upon it. For no one can lay a foundation other than that which is laid, which is Jesus Christ. Now if anyone builds on the foundation with gold, silver, precious stones, wood, hay, straw—each one's work will become manifest, for the Day will disclose it, because it will be revealed by fire, and the fire will test what sort of work each one has done. If the work that anyone has built on the foundation survives, he will receive a reward. If anyone's work is burned up, he will suffer loss, though he himself will be saved, but only as through fire. (1 Cor. 3:10–15)

On the day of judgment, individual pastors will give an account before God for the souls they oversee (Heb. 13:17), even as they serve with other elders. And individual preachers will equally give an account for their teaching, even as a church may have multiple elders who can teach (see James 3:1 and 5:14). That is to say, it will not fly on the day of judgment to declare, "The sermon team that you gave me offered me the manuscript and I ate." No, teaching pastors have a unique calling to deliver the Word of God and stand accountable for it. This is why plagiarism in the pulpit is so disqualifying and why the use of sermon teams must be carefully considered.

In the case of Ed Litton, I *do not* want to conjecture. Instead, I *do* want to give him the benefit of the doubt on his use of a sermon team. Even more, in this chapter, I want to do more than rail against sermon teams. I want to argue for the best way to employ them. In what follows, I will consider what a sermon team is in its popular vernacular. Then, from Scripture, I will argue for what a sermon team ought to be—namely, a fraternity of qualified elders. Let's start with a modern description and then move to a biblical prescription. Along the way, I will show why the postmodern traits of many sermon teams need to be replaced with the superior traits of biblical elders.

WHAT IS A SERMON TEAM?

In an interview with Sermonary, a sermon-building software platform, Litton describes how to create a "preaching team."[48] In that interview, he explains some of the ways his eight-person team works. By and large, he states that his team seeks to invest in other preachers. He says "there are several reasons" for building a preaching team:

> First, it's important because we're supposed to replicate ourselves—that's part of disciple-making. It's also about raising up the next generation. We all have an expiration date, but some of us are a lot closer than others. And I think this is a serious issue, because it's very hard for our church to find good personnel. There are services out there, we've used those. We've searched relationally and connection-ally, but honestly? We should raise them up from

within so that they have our church's DNA. It also fits into our strategy for planting other campuses or "gospel outposts." Gospel outposts are gatherings that would never be self-sufficient or self-supporting, but they need the Word.[49]

Laying aside the biblical problems associated with multiple campuses, the future-oriented nature of Litton's sermon teams is good. Faithful pastors *should* be raising up future preachers. And faithful churches *should* support the training and calling of biblically qualified pastors. Thus, in Litton's answer, we find a positive good in building preaching teams. At the same time, we also find the reverse.

If Litton is influencing the next generation, they are also influencing him. In his interview, Litton suggests that his "verbiage" needs the help and correction of younger ministers. He points to a student minister "who's got the guts to look at you and say, 'I wouldn't use that word.'"[50] While acknowledging the goodness of learning from others, if there is an underlying problem with the use of sermon teams, it is the slide toward postmodernism, where lived experience overrides biblical authority.

Without wandering too far into a study on postmodernism, it is interesting to hear the way Litton illustrates his point. He states,

> When new words are used, or when words change meaning on us and we don't really catch that, you need a student pastor who's got the guts to look at you and say, "I wouldn't use that word." Once I was

> preaching on a very sensitive sexual topic, and my student pastor said to me, "That was great, but watch your tone." I said, "Tone? Really?" but I did. And I got more written responses to that message than I've ever gotten, and every single one of the [sic] said, "Thank you for your tone."[51]

The postmodern turn here is both subtle and significant—and it may not even be discernible to Litton or those who have come to his defense. But here it is: Litton's appeal to youth puts the authority of language in the perspective of the younger minister instead of the Scripture itself. While it may seem innocuous to prefer the language of youth, especially if you seeking to reach a younger audience, this appeal to language is downstream from postmodern ideas. Postmodernism accomplishes much of its efficacy by replacing traditional terms with new ones. Similarly, it elevates the sentiments of the community over and above any historical and/or transcendent truth. Intentionally or not, this deference to communal speech is exactly what sermon teams invite.

Whereas biblical Christianity has always regarded Scripture as the final authority (think *sola Scriptura*), the use of sermon teams invites the authority of the group to shade the text. To make myself clear: I do not think that Litton or churches who use sermon teams intend to put themselves over the text. But, as Marshall McLuhan has famously quipped, "the medium is the message."[52] And given the fact that many contemporary preachers—evangelical preachers, no less—believe that one's experience is what gives them the right to speak about a subject, it is not surprising that sermons teams are springing up and that postmodern hermeneutics are infiltrating "Bible" churches. Consider: Why are women preaching Mother's Day sermons? Why must an older man preach on parenting? Or why does an older man need a younger man to redefine his language? The answer is that experience has often become more important than exposition.

Now, it is true that life experience can give one greater understanding, but only if such experience is submitted to the Word of God. If life experience is informed by worldly philosophies (e.g., feminism, critical race theory, or any other critical theory), then age only exacerbates the problem. When we see unbiblical ideologies being fused with Scripture, then we should retreat to the words of Psalm 119:97–100:

> Oh how I love your law! It is my meditation all the day. Your commandment makes me wiser than my enemies, for it is ever with me. I have more understanding than all my teachers, for your testimonies are my meditation. I understand more than the aged, for I keep your precepts.

If Scripture is our guide, we cannot say that lived experience *necessarily* improves our understanding or our preaching. The man steeped in Scripture who has not experienced parenthood is better equipped to speak to fathers and mothers than the grandfather whose parenting has been formed by sitcoms and psychologists. And the man who has read his Bible is more informed about biblical womanhood than the woman who hasn't.[53] If this is shocking, it only shows how deep the rot of postmodern thought goes. We all need our minds renewed *by the Word of God* and by those who are steeped in Scripture, not simply those who are made experts by lived experience.

Here is how this applies to preaching: Sermon teams are only as good as the men and women(?) who make them up.[54] As I will argue below, there is a good and healthy place for pastors to get input from others. Preachers are not omni-sapient when it comes to preaching the Bible. Yet far better is the solitary preacher who studies the unchanging Word of God than the man who is beholden to the ever-changing views of others.

Returning to the point, there exists today in our postmodern world a denigration of authority. This is true in the church, in families, in the public square, and everywhere else we look. If a sermon team works to craft messages that are more sensitive—since the lived experience can better shape the tone of a text—instead of letting the tone come from the text itself, then we have entered a place where the authority of Scripture is compromised. And with that compromise comes the compromise of the preached Word and God's plan for pulpit ministry.

From a certain angle, there is a downgrade of God's authority when the message is overly finessed by the tone police of a sermon team. A sermon team might assist the pastor in not putting his foot in his mouth, but if he is a man of God steeped in the Scriptures, this should not be a persistent problem. The problem is that far too many churches do not have pastors steeped in the Word. Thus, they must compensate by developing teams—a trend that is of a piece with borrowing sermons.

Ultimately, each sermon team must be evaluated on its own merits (or demerits), but lest we think that the medium does not affect the message, it is important to see how a team approach to sermons fits well in our community-oriented, authority-escaping, postmodern world. As good as it is to study the Word in community (see the next section), there is a danger of fostering multi-perspectival, truth-by-committee, hyper-sensitive preaching. When that happens, the authority of the Word, the sermon, and the preacher are compromised. Thus, we need to resist this trend. In its place, we need to recover a biblical understanding of "sermon teams" that are composed of individual elders who form a fraternity of preachers.

The Goodness of Sermon Teams

The problem of relying on the work of others cannot be laid at the feet of any one pastor. In recent days, multiple websites, blogs, and videos have called for pastors to *preach* less and *share* more. Within this trend, there are healthy observations and exhortations, and there are unhealthy admonitions and applications. Let's consider both as we move closer to what Scripture says.

To get a sense of the current situation, consider The Rocket Company, a ministry dedicated to helping churches and their budgets grow.[55] In one of their YouTube videos, they argue for the need to create a preaching team.[56] Their argument is generally pragmatic. As their video presentation puts it, there are "three secrets to building the best sermon team." These include (1) getting better at preaching, (2) avoiding burnout in ministry, and (3) fulfilling your mission.[57]

Similarly, Ministry Pass, "a teaching resource and multimedia service for pastors," argues "Why a Preaching Team Makes You Better (And How to Build One)."[58] In their podcast, *Hello Church!*, they explain why preaching teams are needed. They suggest that a preaching team, made of multiple voices, brings balance to the pulpit; provides experience for younger preachers; and protects the lead pastor from being the only communicator in the church.[59]

Again, this team approach to preaching can be healthy for the preacher and the church. Such goodness, however, depends upon preachers continuing to study the Word of God on their own. Preaching teams cannot be replacements for personal study. At best, they are sounding boards for sifting ideas and catalysts for incorporating good habits for preaching.[60]

Finally, Joel Brooks from Harbor Media presents what may be the best case for sermon teams. In his article "9 Reasons Why Lead Pastors Should Preach Less," he explains the goodness of sharing the pulpit.[61] Below are his nine reasons, summarized. ("A shared pulpit" is my language).

1. A shared pulpit . . . avoids turning the pastor into a celebrity.
2. A shared pulpit . . . encourages lay elders in the church.
3. A shared pulpit . . . "attacks the consumer mentality."
4. A shared pulpit . . . permits other preachers to flourish.
5. A shared pulpit . . . helps pastors to learn from others and to model learning.
6. A shared pulpit . . . is biblical, as churches are called to have a plurality of elders.
7. A shared pulpit . . . enables other elders to gain an appreciation for the call to preach.
8. A shared pulpit . . . blesses the preacher's wife.
9. A shared pulpit . . . blesses the pastor with rest.

For all these reasons, there is much goodness from having a team approach to preaching. In my church, I am restricted each year to preaching 75 percent of the time. The genesis of this stems from events that occurred at our church before my arrival, many of which echo the points listed by Joel Brooks. So I would commend a team approach to filling the pulpit. However, I would strongly discourage a team approach to individual sermons.

As outlined in the previous chapters, pastors are called to use their gift of teaching by means of studying the Word on their own and then bringing their own message to the people. Of course, a pastor will rely on the insights of others. Authors, commentators, fellow elders, and members of the pastor's church and family will inevitably provide insight into the Word and the world. Still, it is the calling of a preacher to deliver the Word of God. A Spirit-filled man is a vehicle for God to speak to his people.

When teams of people develop individual sermons, however, personal responsibility is eroded and the ongoing ministry of the qualified elder is compromised. Moreover, the authority of God's Word, which is upheld by the servant of the Word, is also compromised. As noted earlier, our postmodern mood invites collaborative sermon-making. Why? Because many chafe at the idea of one man standing before a group of diverse people and letting that man have the only voice. But that is exactly what preaching is. When we let the Bible define preaching, we find a pattern of individual elders teaching sound doctrine and reproving error. These men must conform to the standards of Scripture (1 Tim. 3:1–7; Titus 1:5–9; 1 Pet. 5:1–4), and they should receive their calling to preach by the authority of a local church. All the same, once we acknowledge the contingent nature of a pastor's calling, we must remember that when he heralds gospel truth, he does so as one speaking from the authority of God's Word.

In our day, such thinking is offensive because (1) it promotes the voice of one individual over the diverse views of various groups, and (2) it affirms patriarchy (because only men are permitted to preach to the gathered church).[62] For these reasons, churches may seek to offer more sensitive sermons by permitting multiple voices to have their say. Even if one man is conveying the information, when the sermon was created by committee, it serves to make the message more palatable. And if the sermon can be turned into a discussion between a pastor and his wife, as some churches have begun promoting, then all the better.

Again, the rationale is postmodern, where authority is vested in the diverse community more than the unchanging Word of God. True, many will not say it this plainly, but methodology that does not have a biblical basis has a way of distorting orthodoxy. Therefore, in a world where diversity and inclusion result in a lowest common denominator consensus, we should make sure that the goodness of studying Scripture in community does not devolve into sermon teams who write sermons by groupthink. That's what I am arguing *against*. What I'm arguing *for* is a biblical approach to building sermon teams.

A BIBLICAL SERMON TEAM: A FRATERNITY OF GIFTED ELDERS

Thus far, I have warned against collaborative efforts in making sermons. That point being made, it is time to turn to the blessings that come from studying Scripture in community and developing a fraternity of gifted teachers. In the rest of this chapter, I will offer a biblical picture of a sermon team—namely, a fraternity of churchmen who are recognized as qualified elders.

In the book of Acts, Paul spent up to three years in Ephesus teaching in the Hall of Tyrannus (19:10; 20:31). As Luke reports it, Paul reasoned daily with the disciples "so that all the residents of Asia heard the word of the Lord, both Jews and Greeks" (Acts 19:10). How did this happen?

Did Paul and his disciples spend time crafting sermons they would preach together? Or did Paul focus his attention on the men he was teaching, with the goal of sending them out to preach? The answer to that question comes from a close inspection of Paul's other letters, especially the three we know as the pastoral epistles.

Putting my cards on the table, I don't think Timothy or Titus were "pastors." Rather, they were evangelists (2 Tim. 4:2), sent by Paul (1 Tim. 1:3) and recalled by Paul (Titus 3:12), who had, by their connection with the apostle, the authority to appoint elders (Titus 1:5) and conduct church discipline (1 Tim. 1:3–11). I am Baptist enough to believe that only churches can recognize or call pastors or issue church discipline, which means that Timothy and Titus enjoyed an apostolic authority that did not continue throughout church history.

In short, Timothy and Titus were not local church pastors, but "apostolic delegates," as the late theologian George Knight and others have put it.[63] Under the auspices of the apostle Paul, these two preachers of the Word were called to teach, reprove, and correct the saints gathered in Ephesus (Timothy) and Crete (Titus). By their ministry of the Word, they were called to set up churches that would have ongoing elders (1 Tim. 3:1–7; Titus 1:5–9) and deacons (1 Tim. 3:8–13).

I bring up Timothy and Titus because they provide a model of the way in which Paul discipled men and then sent them out. In his second letter to Timothy, Paul explains his reasons. Thinking of future ministers and those whom they will teach, Paul says to Timothy, "And what you have heard from me in the presence of many witnesses entrust to faithful men, who will be able to teach others also" (2:2). In this verse, we get a picture of how Paul partnered with others in preaching. Namely, he invested his life and doctrine into Timothy so that Timothy could do the same. In principle, this is what is known as spiritual multiplication. And it is worlds apart from sermon teams crafting sermons together. It is focused on the men who will be made, not the sermons that will be preached.

So in Ephesus, Paul spent three years teaching. As a result, Luke offers a terse but telling description—"all the residents of Asia heard the word of the Lord" (Acts 19:10). Why did they hear? First, it was because God sovereignly permitted the hearing of the Word. Remember, the Holy Spirit had previously resisted Paul's attempts to go to Asia (Acts 16:6). So God is sovereign over where and how his Word is preached. Secondarily, the Word went out to Asia because it seems that Paul sent preachers into all the villages around Ephesus. If the pattern we find with Timothy and Titus holds up, then we can reasonably conclude that Paul trained men who, in turn, taught others the Word of God. Ephesus was the hub city from which a powerful gospel witness radiated.

Therefore, we find in Paul a commitment to team teaching, but such teaching is focused on the raising up of teachers more than the production of sermons. This point needs to be grasped in full. For, in addition to being swayed by the influences of postmodernism, the modern church has become beholden to consumerism.

Such consumerism shows up in the way multi-site churches are built upon the charisma of one gifted teacher and why those same mega-churches employ video feeds at each of their "campuses." Moreover, when churches sell a certain "brand," they have to do quality control. At the risk of being overly cynical, having a sermon team is one way to protect the brand and to ensure the right DNA. If a team of pastors in multiple campuses studies the same text and follows the same outline, it ensures that the product is generally the same in each franchise. At first, this approach may seem wise and effective. But notice how individual accountability is lost in the process.

Additionally, a team approach to filling the pulpit may have the positive effect of fighting the idea of pastor as celebrity, but that doesn't mean it is impervious to consumerism. For example, when the goal of a sermon team is to build a product that goes by the name of a "sermon," the focus can easily fall upon the packaging of a message more than the holiness of the preacher—or the development of future preachers. When the sermon is the thing, life and doctrine can be lost.

Here's the point: A healthy team approach should include and equip men who are gifted to preach so that *the men* are better prepared for a life of ministry. By contrast, an unhealthy team crafts sermons that one man, or a team of campus pastors, will preach, with less regard for training and launching pastors to other places. Do you see the difference?

From the outside looking in, it might be difficult to know what the aims of a sermon team are. It might equally be difficult to discern whether the stated intentions match the long-term fruit. But from a comparison with Scripture, we can make a plain distinction. Healthy sermon teams are a fraternity of biblical qualified elders (or aspiring elders) who spur each other on to improve their handling of the Word. Part of that spurring on includes a commitment to rebuking one another if they start to get lazy in their study or overly committed to the voices of men, instead of the Word of God.

To summarize all that I have said, let me offer these seven points:

1. A biblical sermon team should be a plurality of biblically qualified elders.
2. A plurality of elders should spur each other on to show themselves approved workmen in the Word (cf. 2 Tim. 2:15).
3. A plurality of elders does not remove the individual responsibility to study or peach faithfully. It reinforces that responsibility.
4. Individual preachers should learn from others.
5. Individual preachers should seek to share the pulpit but not their sermons.
6. Excepting the mutual call to prayer, the sermon is not a team effort.
7. The team effort is in found in a fraternity of preachers who celebrate the gospel being preached by one

another, without plagiarizing or depending upon the work of another.

As Paul says in Romans 14, every man must give an account for his own work and his own conscience. Pastors, above all others, should model glad-hearted fraternity among their fellow preachers. Even when we may hold different views or different styles of preaching, we should celebrate those who preach the gospel honestly and earnestly (Phil 1:16).

At the same time, we should not forget that we will give an account for every word that we speak (Matt. 12:36). For that reason, the words we speak should be our own and not the fabrication of someone else. If the words we say come from the heart (12:34), it is vital that we *preach* words that come from our hearts—hearts purified by the Word. Plagiarizing sermons and preaching messages formed in committee cannot do that, and so we return to the plea of this book: Brothers, we are not plagiarists. Preach the Word with your own words.

Chapter 5

Annotations and Allusions

BEST PRACTICES FOR PREACHING LIKE THE APOSTLES

In his book *What the Dog Saw and Other Adventures,* the pundit and provocateur Malcolm Gladwell offers the best defense for plagiarism I have seen.[64] Or, at least, he asks questions about plagiarism that far exceed the justifications offered by various pastors. The only qualification for his defense, however, is that what Gladwell describes is not plagiarism at all. Rather, it is simply the way literature, lyrics, and lessons from Scripture are—or should be—formed. There is, in Gladwell's words, a difference between "borrowing that is transformative" and "borrowing that is merely derivative."[65] Applied to sermons, there is a difference between crafting a message with appropriate dependence on others and merely copying a sermon with or without proper attribution.[66]

In his essay "Something Borrowed: Should a Charge of Plagiarism Ruin Your Life?" Gladwell identifies a Broadway play where the characters, stories, language, and so on were taken from the work of a noted psychologist. This revelation led to a lawsuit, which led to Gladwell's meditation on creativity. As he always does, Gladwell amplifies the ambiguities of the case and makes the reader question whether or not the playwright should have been sued for copyright infringement. Along the way, he considers how musicians regularly borrow from others. And, recalling a conversation with someone "who works in the music industry," he makes the following point:

> My friend had hundreds of these examples [i.e., artists borrowing from other artists]. We could have sat in his living room playing at musical genealogy for hours. Did the examples upset him? Of course not, because he knew enough about music to know that these patterns of influence—cribbing, tweaking, transforming—were at the very heart of the creative process. True, copying could go too far. There were times when one artist was simply replicating the work of another, and to let that pass inhibited true creativity. But it was equally dangerous to be overly vigilant in policing creative expression . . .[67]

Here is the rub. Songs or, in our case, sermons that are mere copies "go too far." This is what we must avoid and eliminate. At the same time, there *are* honest and healthy ways to "borrow" from others.[68] Applied to sermons, good preachers will often utilize a public-domain quotation or a literary turn of phrase without identifying its origin. In a recent sermon, I offered an imaginative illustration (not a personal anecdote) that was inspired by the real-life experience of another preacher. This is not copying—it is creativity. Over time, seasoned preachers will learn how to salt their expositions with echoes from the Bible, theology, poetry, and popular culture—note the possessive pronoun "their" there.

These borrowed words should flavor the sermon in a way that gives the congregation a taste for the Word of God and the truths being communicated therein. This kind of "borrowing that is transformative" is wholly different from the other kind of "borrowing that is merely derivative." Or to riff on Gladwell, there is a difference between *creative borrowing*, where the preacher is crafting his own words with the help of others, and *repetitive borrowing*, where the preacher is merely reusing the words of others. I am not going to quantify this difference, as if to say that a sermon with 95 percent original material is acceptable while a sermon with 85 percent is not. But the point remains: There is an important distinction between creating and copying.

In the previous chapters, I have made the case for why mere copying (re-tweeting, if you will) is unbiblical and destructive for the ministry of the Word. In what follows, I will attempt to balance my argument against that kind of borrowing with a positive form of borrowing that is honest, healthy, and wholesome. Indeed, this kind of borrowing is both biblical and unavoidable. In fact, with our minds fixed on the Bible's prophets and preachers, we can find a biblical approach to crafting sermons that avoid plagiarism, on the one hand, *and* the paralysis caused by a fear of plagiarism, on the other. Thus, in searching for a wise appropriation of words (e.g., ideas, illustrations, and applications), we need to consider (1) the textured nature of the text, (2) the power of the Word preached, and (3) the best practices for citing the Bible and other voices.

THE TEXTURED NATURE OF THE TEXT

If we are going to think rightly about using words, we should begin with the Word. And in the Bible, we discover that every word is the product of two authors—the human author and the divine. From the start, therefore, we must admit that our words about the Word (sermons) possess a different nature from Scripture's words. While Christ speaks through the Spirit-filled preacher, such speaking is qualitatively different from the speech of the prophets and apostles, whose very words were the result of the Spirit's work (see 2 Tim. 3:16; 2 Pet. 1:21). This caveat in place, we can look to the authors of Scripture, especially the New Testament apostles, as models for preaching.

For every prophet after Moses, the truthfulness of the speaker is dependent upon previous revelation and the appropriate reuse of their words. As Deuteronomy 13 and 18 detail, if a prophet deviates from the Law, he is false and subject to death. And in the rest of the Bible, every true prophet, including Jesus Christ, proves their faithfulness by how they handle, depend upon, quote, and apply the Law and the Prophets (cf. Luke 24:27; John 5:39).

As a result, every part of the Bible sounds like every other part of the Bible. That is to say, though Isaiah's voice is not the same as Ezekiel's and John puts things differently than Matthew, there remains a common vocabulary and pattern of speech among the biblical authors. Thinking theologically, this comes from the one divine Author breathing out every word of Scripture. But it also comes from human authors who depended upon other human authors. From this practice, we find that both Testaments are filled with citations, allusions, and echoes to other, earlier, or even contemporary parts of Scripture. Consider the way Daniel reads Jeremiah (Dan. 9:2) or the way Paul cites Luke (1 Tim. 5:18). In Scripture, the authors regularly depend on one another.

Therefore, we find in the Bible a multi-layered book, a textured text. And one of the ways that Scripture teaches us to live, and move, and have our preaching is to take up the patterns of speech in Scripture and weave them into our own. Did you see what I did there? Compare that last sentence to Acts 17:28. It is not plagiarism to "riff" on the words of others. It is part of what it means to be human, living in a world that depends upon the traditions and texts of earlier humans.

To show this point more fully, look at Acts 17:24–29. In his sermon to the philosophers on Mars Hill, Paul quotes two poet-philosophers of his day. One he references in general, the other he does not. Prior to these quotations, he also alludes (without attribution) to multiple passages from the

Old Testament. Here is the passage with the allusions and quotations set in brackets.[69]

> The God who made the world and everything in it [Neh. 9:6], being Lord of heaven and earth, does not live in temples made by man [1 Kings 8:27], nor is he served by human hands [Isa. 66:1], as though he needed anything, since he himself gives to all mankind life and breath and everything [Isa. 42:5]. And he made from one man every nation of mankind to live on all the face of the earth, having determined allotted periods and the boundaries of their dwelling place [Deut. 32:8–9, which refers to Genesis 10–11], that they should seek God, and perhaps feel their way toward him and find him. Yet he is actually not far from each one of us, for "In him we live and move and have our being" [Epimenides of Crete?]; as even some of your own poets have said, "For we are indeed his offspring" [Aratus of Soli]. Being then God's offspring, we ought not to think that the divine being is like gold or silver or stone, an image formed by the art and imagination of man.

Do you see what Paul is doing? He is flavoring his sermon at Mars Hill with the ancient Scriptures and the modern philosophers of his day. And more than just flavoring for flavoring sake, he is thickening his argument for the supremacy of God, in a world worshiping multiple deities, with the words of others.

Because our focus is on form, not content, we will limit our observations to *how* Paul speaks. (Or at least how Luke records his speech). Notice that, in these six verses, Paul cites his sources inconsistently. Sometimes he calls attention to his quotation, sometimes not. What I am going to argue is that this sermon clip from Acts 17 is representative of the whole Bible.

As two recent reference works point out, both the Old Testament prophets and the New Testament apostles depend heavily on other authors of Scripture.[70] Never in Scripture do they provide endnotes, and only sometimes do they cite their sources directly. If Scripture is our guide, then, this practice of citing Scripture sometimes and alluding other times is a starting place for understanding how to preach God's Word without plagiarizing. But this assumes a commitment to preaching the Word where the power of the Word, not the power of preacher, is upheld.

THE POWER IS IN THE WORD PREACHED,
NOT THE PREACHER OF THE WORD

Highlighting the distinction between the power of the Word and the power of the preacher, pastor Bryan Chapell reminds preachers that the power of preaching is not the man preaching, but the Word preached. After citing text after text to show the power of God's Word,[71] he concludes,

> Scripture's portrayal of its own potency challenges us always to remember that *the Word preached* rather than the *preaching of the Word* accomplishes

heaven's purposes. Preaching that is true to Scripture converts, convicts, and conforms the spirit of men and women because it presents the instrument of divine compulsion, not because preachers have any transforming power in themselves.[72]

While subtle, the distinction between *the Word preached* and *the preaching of the Word* is seismic. It is the continental divide between two kinds of preachers—the one who can go to sleep knowing God's Word will work (Mark 4:26–29) and the other who cannot go to sleep because he's not sure his sermon will work (Psalm 127:2). Hence, the temptation to borrow someone else's.

To press this further, the Word-centered preacher will trust the Word and the Spirit to produce their God-given effect (see 1 Thess. 1:5–10). As a result, his sermon will reflect the greater realities of God and his heart will rest in prayerful faith. By contrast, the sermon-centered preacher will be tempted to impress people with his oration. In circles where the preacher is too highly exalted, the church, the ministry, and the man himself may begin to think that he is indispensable and irreplaceable. Such is the logic that undergirds many multi-site churches with video campuses. But to this way of thinking, we must ask: Where is the confidence? Is it in the peddler of the Word or in the Word of God preached?

Certainly, every man must give an account for his teaching (James 3:1), and those who labor in their studies can do so for the praises of men, while those who use the sermons of others can convince themselves they are doing it for the glory of God. But leaving inner motivations to the Lord, we can say, objectively, that our theology will impact our practices. If we are committed to the content of Scripture, we should also be committed to its form. Thus, for those who seek to preach the Word faithfully, we should learn from the Word how the inspired apostles treated the words of others.

FOUR WAYS TO PREACH LIKE THE APOSTLES

The question of how the apostles used the Old Testament is massive. Entire books have been written on how one author picks up one theme from the Old Testament.[73] Acknowledging the vastness of this subject, I am simply going to suggest four ways the apostles "annotated" their work. The first two—(1) citing and (2) alluding—are the two practices we find in Scripture. Then, the second two—(3) selective name dropping and (4) communities of the Word—are the two processes that the practices depend upon.

All told, these four apostolic habits are not the only things we could glean from Scripture, but they begin to make us aware that to plagiarize or not is not simply a (post)modern decision. Instead, Scripture models for us a way of handling the words of others. And while there is a certain measure of freedom in citing others, that freedom is found in obedience to the Law ("Do not steal"), not in freedom from the Law. So let's learn how the apostles handled the words of others, and see how we might imitate their faithfulness (cf. 1 Cor. 4:16).

Citations. First of all, the apostles regularly cite Scripture. That is to say, in order to make their arguments, they say things like "as it is written" (Acts 15:15) or "as it is written in the book of the prophets" (7:42) or "for David says concerning [Christ]" (2:25) or "as the Holy Spirit says" (Heb. 3:7). In all of these, James, Stephen, Peter, and the author of Hebrews, respectively, make their points by pointing to the text of Scripture.[74] In fact, this last citation from Hebrews comes from a book-length sermon that shows what biblical exposition looks like in the Bible. Again, without drawing this out too far, the first point to observe is the fact that biblical preachers cite the Bible.

By application, we should remember that an apostolic sermon is one that regularly quotes, applies, and explains other parts of the Bible. Not surprisingly— or maybe it is surprising— a biblical sermon must be filled with the Bible. This is not just an idea that comes after the Bible. It is what we find *in the Bible*. It teaches us that we should cite Scripture in our sermons, and that we should let people know that we are citing Scripture.

By extension, it is appropriate to cite other quotations, facts, and illustrations, if and when we want to drive people to those voices. Certainly, one of the goals of a sermon is to point people back to the Bible, and the same must be true when we name the commentators, theologians, and pastors who help us understand the Bible. It is honest and healthy to "name drop" in a sermon. Yet we should be intentional about our name dropping, which is to say we have options when we quote. (We will talk more about this shortly.)

Sometimes, we may quote something and give the name of the author. Other times, however, we might simply say "as one Old Testament scholar has said" if that author is less than reliable in all that he says. For instance, I might quote someone like the Old Testament scholar John Walton in a sermon, but because of his views on inerrancy, I may not want to say his name. In the context of that sermon, it unintentionally endorses him when, in fact, I would want to differentiate the parts of his theology I appreciate and those I reject. Of course, in quoting Scripture, we do not find this practice. But in our sermons we will. And this leads to the last kind of quotation—namely, quoting without naming.

Now I realize this concession may seem to contradict my whole argument, and I think that there can be differences of conscience here, but here is the rule of thumb: When you preach a sermon and you incorporate a line—not a paragraph, not a page, but a line—from someone else, you are not plagiarizing if you do not give his or her name. This is especially true if you incorporate Scripture, a famous quotation, or even an unknown sentence from someone and make a part of their sentence your own. Such incorporation approximates Gladwell's "borrowing that is transformative," and this leads to the next way Scripture "cites" itself.[75]

Allusions. Getting back to the Bible, there is another way Scripture refers to itself. In addition to citing with or without a name, the Bible regularly "alludes" to other parts of the Bible. According to some counts, there may be anywhere between 600 and 4,100 allusions in the Bible.[76] Biblical theologian G. K. Beale, who gives these numbers, defines allusions as "indirect references" or "brief expression[s] consciously intended by an author to be dependent on an OT passage."[77] When it comes to preaching, we should learn from biblical preachers how to make allusions.

For instance, the apostles often allude to earlier parts of Scripture. We saw this practice in Acts 17, and I would argue that nearly every paragraph of the New Testament borrows something from the Old. In fact, God quotes himself when he introduces the Son at Jesus's baptism. In Matthew 3:17 we find these words: "And behold, a voice from heaven said, 'This is my beloved Son, with whom I am well pleased.'" Remarkably, without citing chapter and verse, God draws language from Genesis 22, Isaiah 42, and Psalm 2 to identify Jesus. Then, he adds another layer in Matthew 17 when, at Jesus's Transfiguration, he adds "listen to him" in verse 5. This last word comes from Deuteronomy 18:15.

Such is the way of our God. What he promises, he fulfills. What he says earlier in Scripture, he echoes later. Even what he says and does later in history has been prepared earlier in Scripture (see, e.g., Gal. 4:4; Heb. 10:1). What this means for the authors of Scripture is that, led by the Holy Spirit, they are regularly speaking words that echo, allude to, and reframe earlier parts of the Bible. This is one way God's preachers authenticate themselves. Moreover, this pattern of "bibline" speech is something preachers should imitate.

As I have learned from pastors who have gone before me, an approach to preaching that sounds like the Bible is more

caught than taught.[78] It is not something you can lift from
the notes of another preacher, but it is what the Spirit does
within the man who has drunk deeply from the Word of
God. Yet when sermons become commodities to be traded,
rather than the personal overflow of a heart brimming with
Bible, it should not surprise us that men take up the words
of others. What we find in the Bible is a commitment to fill
our words with the words of God, and this results in preachers whose speech echoes Scripture.

Simultaneously, because we preach in places and times,
we can and should engage the congregation with words
that dip into the leaf mold of language. As Douglas Wilson
points out, referring to J.R.R Tolkien, "His ideas sprang
up from the leaf mold of his mind."[79] In other words, the
words we use in our sermons should often include allusions
from, echoes of, and riffs on culture. Like Paul in Athens,
we should take up the stuff of the world and turn it back on
those who are lost so that they can find the light for which
they are looking.

In such instances, you may not say the name of the person
you are citing. Or you might. It depends on what you are
trying to accomplish with the inclusion of the name, which
is the third point.

When you name drop, know why you are doing it. We do not
have to annotate everything we quote in a sermon so long as
(1) we are citing a verse or a sentence, not a paragraph or a
page, (2) we are putting quotes or allusions into our message
and not making someone else's message our own, or (3)

what we are saying is so well known that saying the name is unnecessary. Pertaining to this third point, we have options when it comes to name dropping, and also challenges.

For instance, we may want to note that it was Martin Luther King Jr. who said, "The arc of the moral universe is long but it bends towards justice," but in America, that would not be necessary. This is a famous quotation, so we do not need to cite it. At the same time, a little digging tells us that this was *not* his quotation after all, but a longstanding aphorism in America. King cited it with quotations, but not attribution, in a speech given in 1964.[80] So here is an example of the way language develops and an instance of the way preachers have liberty to say the name, or not. Learning when and how to "name drop," therefore, is important for good preaching and something that Scripture models for us as well.

Considering the previous examples, there are places where names are added, but, in other places, one might simply say, "It has been testified somewhere" (Heb. 2:6; cf. 4:4). Good preachers do the same. As one fellow said, "If the expression [you are citing] is distinctive, but you don't want to look like you live in Footnoteville, [preach], 'As the fellow said.'"[81] I trust you get the point.

So, on the one hand, don't copy someone else's work when you preach the Bible, and on the other, don't make it look like you are citing everything you read. If you don't know how to make up your mind on what to cite or not, just stick to the Bible. The Bible is public domain, or it used to be. And it should be the place where we get most of our expositions, illustrations, and applications. Indeed, observant students of the Word and the world don't need illustration books. Illustrations are everywhere. Moreover, if the Bible is the primary source of your sermon, you will make your people read their Bibles, which brings about the fourth and last feature of biblical preaching without plagiarizing.

Communities of the Word. When you preach in church, you should know that you are not alone. For not only do you have the Holy Spirit leading you, but you also have the assembled saints praying for you and testifying with you that the Word is true. This latter point, the congregation's role in the Word preached, is often overlooked. Yet when church is not turned into a spectator sport, the active listening of the congregation stands at the heart of biblical preaching.

In the Old Testament, Israel verified the words of the prophets (Deuteronomy 13 and 18). And in the New Testament, Paul commended the Bereans for checking his words with Scripture (Acts 17:11). Moreover, he charged the churches in Galatia to know the true gospel (Gal. 1:6–9), and he expected the churches in Crete (Titus 1:5–9) and Ephesus (1 Tim. 3:1–7) to be able to identify sound teachers. In short, the burden of faithful preaching is not on the pastor alone; it is also on the church. A healthy pulpit ministry is one where the people know and are coming to know God's Word, such that the preacher's allusions to Scripture will in time be understood, appreciated, and enjoyed.

Today, preaching has become such a show that most congregations do not see themselves as needing to give the "amen" to the Word preached. This "amen" is not stylistic or cultural. It is doctrinal. God intends for the gathered church to play a part in the preaching of the Word, and this means demanding that the Word is preached and holding account-able those shepherds who fail to do so. In short, if plagiarism in the pulpit is accepted, the onus for such a practice is on local churches, too.

Stressing the role that churches play in preaching, D. Mar-tyn Lloyd-Jones laments that so many congregations have neglected their duty in preaching. He writes, "The trouble is that so many do not stop to think about such matters"—namely, the way the congregation's failure to participate in the service affects the efficacy of the Word preached.[82]

> [Church members] just go to the service as a mat-ter of duty, and having done so feel better because they have done their duty. That attitude to a service obviously expresses itself and visitors sense this and draw the conclusion that there is not much value in it if this is the attitude of the regular attenders. But, conversely, when they enter a place of worship where people attend because they feel that God meets them there, this also will transmit itself to them in some strange way that one does not quite understand. So they will feel that something real is happening, and it may well be used of God to bring them to a knowledge of the truth.[83]

Apparently, consumerism in the church is not new. But neither is it acceptable just because it is commonplace. Thus, as we consider plagiarism in the pulpit and urge pastors to do the work of the ministry, we must also call churches to hold their pastors accountable and to celebrate the faithful preaching of God's Word. While pastors must not peddle the Word, churches must not tolerate peddlers. It goes both ways. And when it comes to plagiarism, could it be that one of the reasons why it can fly in the church today is that so many churches are biblically illiterate, theologically anemic, and entertainment-oriented?

This book cannot answer that question. But it does point in that direction. If pastors who are plagiarizing sermons are accepted, platformed, defended, and called upon to lead denominations, the problem is not limited to the pastor. So as we wind down this book about pastors plagiarizing in the pulpit, we must also call for churches to be true communities of the Word. The only way peddlers of the Word can continue is if their churches are aiding and abetting the act. What I am calling for here is for pastors and churches to return to the Bible and to be all that Paul describes in 1 Timothy 3—overseers who are above reproach and households of faith that are pillars and buttresses of the truth.

With the true church in view, let me offer five final words of exhortation on best practices for preaching without plagiarizing.

BEST PRACTICES ON PREACHING AND PLAGIARISM

If Malcolm Gladwell's essay on plagiarism is the best defense of borrowing words creatively, then Douglas Wilson's book on writing may be the best practical guide for writing sermons that borrow but do not steal.[84] Thus, I close out this chapter with three of Wilson's reflections and two of my own.

1. "The [preacher's] life is a scavenger's life."[85]

If you are called to regular ministry of the Word, you will need to read, and read, and look, and read some more, in order to fill your mind with truth.[86] This begins with the Bible, continues with books about the Bible, and moves on to encompass all of life. Preachers need to fill their minds with goodness, truth, and beauty. If they do not, the tempting morsel of a stolen sermon will look awfully sweet. Thus, the best way to avoid plagiarism is not *not* reading; it is reading so much that words of life burst from your chest.

Tragically, the ubiquitous sermon series based upon movies and other cultural events—"Fifty Shades of Grace" (barf!)—is a warning to the church that her pastors are filling their minds with *something*, but that something is not the Word of God. Why are our churches so weak? Could it be that the men standing in the pulpit are scavenging the wrong things? Brothers, we must feed on the Word constantly to feed the flock faithfully.

2. "It is dishonest to take the wit and wisdom of others and represent it as your own."[87]

Imagine if this simple, biblical aphorism would be applied by every preacher. It would spare the church much grief and it would begin to rebuild a reputation for pastors. At the same time, pastors need not pretend that every thought originated with them. Speaking to writers, Wilson continues, "It is not dishonest to have your expressions reflect the fact that you have spent a great deal of time with witty, wise people."[88]

The same applies to preachers: It is not dishonest to have your expositions reflect the fact that you have spent a great deal of time with the Wisdom of God. Indeed, the church needs to know that its pastor has spent time in God's Word. We can add that it is healthy that congregations know who their pastors are reading. If J. I. Packer can say of John Piper that the ghost of Jonathan Edwards is found among the pages of *Desiring God*,[89] it is just another reminder that faithful pastors will bear the marks of others.

In the short term and the long, what a pastor is reading—what he is feeding on—will show. What is done, or not done, in the study will come into the light. And the church needs the light that comes from pastors who do not steal but who labor in the text.

3. "To quote others is to demonstrate that you are listening. If you have modified the phrase, you have made it your own, which you have the authority to do. If you did not modify it, or did not modify it significantly, then you should in some way acknowledge it as the contribution of another person in the conversation."[90]

Applying this principle to the whole sermon, pastors should be inspired by the work of others, but they should never be the mouthpiece of another preacher. Simply acknowledging that a pastor preached another's sermon does not make it right. Instead, it invites all the problems outlined in this book. Therefore, pastors, and those who aspire to preach, should vow before the Lord to preach the Word of God with their own words. As Charles Spurgeon has said, "In order that you may impress the Word upon those to whom you preach, remember that it must be impressed upon yourself first. You must feel it yourself, and speak as a man who feels it, not *as if* you feel it, but *because* you feel it, otherwise you will not make it felt by others."[91]

The church needs more than impressive preachers. It needs, as I once heard David Helm quip, preachers on whom the Word of God has been impressed. May God take this debacle of plagiarism to refine his church and raise up such Word-impressed men.

4. Use endnotes to capture your sources.

Getting more practical, if ever you turn a preached word into a written word, you will want to make sure you do not make the mistake of accidentally making someone else's words your own.[92] It is one thing to preach a sermon and not give attribution to someone's else sentence. It is another thing entirely when you put it in print. The same commandment—the eighth one—applies to spoken and written words, but the standard of precision is increased in writing. Therefore, always endnote your sermons. This practice will largely protect you from plagiarizing in print.

And if, by some strange turn of events, you do find that a spoken word becomes a printed word and that the latter fails to properly attribute your source—admit it. When error is brought to light, confess it and seek to correct it. Charles Spurgeon, Douglas Wilson, and others are good models of this. We should not shy away from confessing sin and ministerial error when it is brought to light.

5. Preach the Word with your words.

As I round out this final chapter, I will finish where I started. Do not be ashamed of the gospel, nor of your calling to hold out the word of truth to those God calls you to pastor. You do not need the slick sermons of others. You have everything you need for life and godliness in the Bible that sits on your desk. Yes, biblical resources must be mined, and such mining takes time to learn. But take heart—preaching the Word is worth it. And laboring to find words that rightly explain and exalt the Word made flesh is worth all your time, effort, and attention.

Do not be deceived or delighted with the fruit offered by the lips of other preachers. Instead, take the food that God himself offers to you. Dwell in the land of the Bible and feed on God's faithfulness. And if you are still struggling to know how to preach the Bible with the resources you have at your disposal, find an older, reliable preacher and learn from him. Don't steal his sermons, but, as Paul said to Timothy, "Practice these things, immerse yourself in them, so that all may see your progress. Keep a close watch on yourself and on the teaching. Persist in this, for by so doing you will save both yourself and your hearers" (1 Tim. 4:15–16).

Indeed, becoming a faithful and enduring preacher takes time. It takes a lifetime. But for those who are willing forsake peddling God's Word, God offers you the true ministry of laboring in his vineyard and shepherding his flock. More than ever, the church needs preachers who tremble before God and his Word (Isa. 66:1–2) and who will stop at nothing to hold forth the Word of God mined from Scripture itself and not from the minds of others.

May we be that kind of preachers, and may we put into practice all the habits we find in Scripture.

> According to the grace of God given to me, like a skilled master builder I laid a foundation, and someone else is building upon it. Let each one take care how he builds upon it. For no one can lay a foundation other than that which is laid, which is Jesus Christ. Now if anyone builds on the foundation with gold, silver, precious stones, wood, hay, straw—each one's work will become manifest, for the Day will disclose it, because it will be revealed by fire, and the fire will test what sort of work each one has done. If the work that anyone has built on the foundation survives, he will receive a reward. If anyone's work is burned up, he will suffer loss, though he himself will be saved, but only as through fire.
>
> 1 Corinthians 3:10–15

Conclusion

On Pragmatism and Plagiarism

A PASTORAL PLEA TO FORSAKE PEDDLING GOD'S WORD

Sermons are a work of creation. Yet, if we are thinking rightly, the power to create a good sermon comes from the gift of the Spirit (Rom. 12:7; 1 Cor. 12:28; Eph. 4:11) and the eternal plans of God (see Eph. 2:10). Thus, no spiritually minded Christian can write a sermon and declare it "mine."[93] Rather, he will acknowledge that his words are not his alone, but Spirit-enabled reflections upon the Word of God (1 Cor. 2:10–16). For this reason, the discussion about plagiarism in the pulpit is not exactly the same as the discussion in the courts of law regarding "property rights." Genuine believers know they have been bought with a price (1 Cor. 6:20) and that every good sermon is a gift from the Father (James 1:17).

At the same time, this "all truth is God's truth" approach to sermons creates another problem—namely, the belief that there is no personal liability associated with sermon-making.[94] While it is true that every good gift comes from God and that God uses means—in this case, pastor-teachers—to communicate his truth to us, this does not mean that sermons are like sportscoats that can be shared if the owner and borrower wear the same size. No, just because we cannot claim property rights on God's truth does not mean we should not hold to some measure of property rights for our sermons.

That is to say, because all Christians should be happy *that* gospel truth goes out does not mean we should be indifferent about *how* it goes out. Gospel advance is not a sufficient argument for passing around well-made sermons. The reason for this is that the sharing of a sermon reeks of self-reliant pragmatism, not God-dependent service.

God *does* care how his Word goes out, and he has written an entire Book to talk about it. Moreover, he cares for the souls of those who are delivering that Word and the souls of those who will hear their preaching. But apparently there are pastors who are not as concerned about the means of communication and how pastors get their material—or at least, that is the ostensible conclusion that comes from letting pastors continue to plagiarize sermons.

In the last year, it has become apparent that there is an entire cottage industry dedicated to putting words into the mouths of preachers, or at least into their notebooks.[95] This is the problem. What is the solution? As I have argued throughout this book, the solution is a return to the biblical standard.

Brothers, we are not plagiarists enslaved to the pragmatism and processes of this world. We are preachers, saved by grace, set free from the world, and sent to the church to preach the truth. If you are called to feed God's flock with the Word of God, then you are called to study and show yourself approved by the Word of God (2 Tim. 2:15).

Too many have settled for peddling God's Word (2 Cor. 2:17), taking the work of others and proclaiming as their own. And too many churches have accepted that and endorsed it. Such low standards are wholly lacking in the Bible. Thus, the final note of this book is one that strikes the chord for revival and repentance.

If you are pastor who has preached the sermons of others, repent. Come clean and stop claiming the work of others as your own. The Lord knows and you know. If you have not labored in the Word but have enjoyed the fruits of God's vineyard, you need to step down. Every individual and every situation will be different. I can't say that every case of plagiarism should result in termination or permanent disqualification. Taking one sermon is different from taking hundreds. But I am saying that serial plagiarism is something that should stop, and a pastor committing such a sin should not preach again until it is resolved. What comes after that is up to the Lord, his people, and the personal, local, and spiritual care of wise saints.

Next, if you are church or a church member who has supported, or permitted, a pastor to plagiarize sermons, repent. Following the standards of 1 Timothy 5:19–20, call your pastor to account. Pastors who are worthy of double honor are those who labor in the Scriptures (1 Tim. 5:17–18). Those who do not labor in the Scripture, but take their work from others, are not worthy of support. Such a statement is serious but, on this matter, so is Scripture. Too many churches are playing games with God's Word, and they need to repent.

Finally, as a denomination, the Southern Baptist Convention needs to repent. There is today a casualness given to the preaching office that permits, defends, and congratulates those pastors who have built large ministries on the words of other men. In this repentance, I am not calling the SBC to make mandates for local churches, or to invite third-party investigators. That is not how Baptists do business. (Because that is not how the Bible orders the church).

I am calling the SBC to resolve to be a denomination that so prizes the Word of God that we would loathe the thought of plagiarism in the pulpit and stop letting leaders who peddle the Word lead our denomination. It is damning that we, as a denomination, can learn of widespread plagiarism in the pulpit and treat it so lightly (Jer. 6:14). We have plenty of leaders who have denounced plagiarism in the abstract, but when we discover plagiarism in form and fact, those same voices are silent. Lord help us! Let us be doers of the Word and not hearers only.

Overall, may the Lord have mercy on all of his churches. And may that mercy begin with a wave of repentance for trading the glories of Scripture and its study for the pre-packaged scripts of others.

Wonderfully, there is grace for those who have peddled the Word, and there is forgiveness for those who have treated preaching so lightly. But such forgiveness is a gift that awaits those who repent. So may God grant us repentance and raise up a generation of preachers who see the pragmatism of sermon plagiarism as the spiritual malpractice that it is. And may God, in his mercy, replace such malpractice with habits of the heart that begin and end in the Bible, such that the Word of God would again be the foundation of the church.

The church is to be the pillar and buttress of the truth, but we can only fulfill that calling when the men who are preaching the Word are doing so with honesty and integrity. May God raise up those men. And may those who are faithfully laboring in the Word be strengthened to persist in that work and not be discouraged by the perceived successes of those who build ministries with the labors of others.

Brother-pastors, we will all give an account for our sermons one day. On that Day of Judgment, the substance of our sermons will be seen for what it is (1 Cor. 3:10–15). So may we be faithful in our peaching today, building always and only upon the foundation of Jesus Christ with the gold, silver, and precious stones that we ourselves have mined from Scripture. For those who do not have the tools to do that, may they be humble enough to step aside so that those with a genuine interest in the work of ministry might study the Scriptures, feed the flock, and tend the lambs.

The church needs true pastors who personally, not professionally, handle the Word with care and conviction. Pastors need churches that will not put up with re-tweeted sermons any longer. May we pray to that end, and may the Lord have mercy and answer our prayers.

Scripture Index

Old Testament

New Testament

Notes

Preface

1 "God-besotted" is a phrase I picked up from Piper, as is the mention of sea shells. For reasons I will explain later, these two references do not necessarily require a footnote, but I add one here to set the record straight—I am, and we all are, dependent on those who have gone before us. Plagiarism is not incorporating words or phrases into our speech that resonate with an established body of literature (or, in this case, sermons). Plagiarism, intentional or not, is when we pass off the ideas of others as our own.

"God-besotted" is the way Piper has often spoken of Jonathan Edwards, who has deeply influenced him. "Seashells" is a reference to Piper's generationally famous sermon illustration preached at Passion 2000. For more, see: "How John Piper's Seashells Swept Over a Generation," The Gospel Coalition, March 20, 2017, https://www.thegospelcoalition.org/article/how-john-pipers-seashells-swept-over-a-generation.

2 These blogs can be found on my website, DavidSchrock.com.

3 John Piper, *Brothers We Are Not Professionals: A Plea to Pastors for Radical Ministry* (Nashville: B & H, 2002). If the distinction between "ripping off" and "riffing on" is unclear, keep reading. We will cover it in chapter 5.

Chapter 1

4 John Piper, "My Pastor Uses Pre-Made Sermons—Should I Be Concerned?" Ask Pastor John, April 4, 2016, https://www.desiringgod.org/interviews/my-pastor-uses-pre-made-sermons-should-i-be-concerned

5 At least one local pastor had the integrity, or audacity, to put a note on his website indicating that not all his sermons were original.

6 Anders Anglesey, "Pastor Ed Litton Removes Over 140 Video Sermons After Being Accused of Plagiarism," *Newsweek*, June 28, 2021, https://www.newsweek.com/pastor-ed-litton-removes-over-140-video-sermons-after-being-accused-plagiarism-1604707; "'Sermongate' Prompts a Quandary: Should Pastors Borrow Words from Another?": *New York Times*, July 6, 2021, https://www.nytimes.com/2021/07/06/us/sermongate-plagiarism-litton-greear.html.

7 Bookman, "Litton and Greear: Borrowing or Plagiarism?" YouTube, https://www.youtube.com/watch?v=l6PJNfbIuS4; Bookman, "Litton and Greear Romans 8:1–11 Sermon Borrowing," YouTube, https://www.youtube.com/watch?v=578d4Z0PV-o&t=203s.

8 J.D. Greear, "A Statement about My Sermon on Romans 1," J.D. Greear Ministries, June 26, 2021, https://jdgreear.com/a-statement-about-my-sermon-on-romans-1; Ed Litton, "Pastor's Statement," Redemption Church, n.d., https://www.goredemption.com/pastors-statement.

9 Anglesey, "Pastor Ed Litton Removes Over 140 Video,"

10 R. Albert Mohler, "Plagiarism in the Pulpit: Stealing the Material We Preach," Albert Mohler, December 7, 2006, https://albertmohler.com/2006/12/07/plagiarism-in-the-pulpit-stealing-the-material-we-preach-2; D. A. Carson, "TGC Asks Don Carson: When Has a Preacher Crossed the Line into Plagiarism in His Sermon?" The Gospel Coalition, December 19, 2010, https://www.thegospelcoalition.org/article/tgc-asks-don-carson-when-has-a-preacher-crossed-the-line-into-plagiarism-in; Piper, "My Pastor Uses Pre-Made Sermons"; Andy Naselli, "On Plagiarism: An Interview with Justin Taylor," December 11, 2015, https://andynaselli.com/on-plagiarism-an-interview-with-justin-taylor.

11 Carson, "TGC Asks Don Carson."

12 SBC Voices, "You Can Preach My Sermon – James Merritt," YouTube, https://www.youtube.com/watch?v=ip_luFFF3K8&t=9s .

13 Here are a few examples: The Docent Group, https://www.docentgroup.com; Ministry Pass, https://ministrypass.com; Lifeway Christian Resources, https://www.lifeway.com/en/articles/pastors-sermon-index-by-scripture.

14 Christianity Today Editorial, "When Pastors Plagiarize," *Christianity Today*, December 9, 2002, https://www.christianitytoday.com/ct/2002/december9/32.29.html.

15 Naselli, "An Interview with Justin Taylor."

16 See TurnItIn.com.

17 "The Plagiarism Spectrum: Instructor Insights into the 10 Types of Plagiarism" https://www.lib.auth.gr/sites/default/files/docs_files/Turnitin_White-Paper_PlagiarismSpectrum.pdf, 4.

18 I am not saying there is no place for Christians to gather and listen to sermons, even written sermons. But I would say this practice is only healthy and good when there is *not* a qualified teacher in their midst. Far better for a poor-but-faithful preacher to preach God's Word than to re-tweet the sermon

of someone else. Likewise, it would be better for a growing preacher to labor in the text and stumble in the pulpit than to be eloquent in the pulpit and stumble with integrity.

19 "When Pastors Plagiarize," 29.

20 Ibid.

21 Ibid.

22 Helmut Thielicke, *A Little Exercise for Young Theologians* (trans. Charles L. Taylor; Grand Rapids: Eerdmans, 1962), 11–12.

23 Haddon W. Robinson, *Biblical Preaching: The Development and Delivery of Expository Messages*, 3rd Ed. (Grand Rapids: Baker Academic, 2014), 14. E-book Edition. Thanks to Bruce Winter for pointing me to Robinson's definition.

24 We will expand on this in chapter 2.

25 We will revisit sermon teams in chapter 4.

26 See, e.g., David Wells, *No Place for Truth: Whatever Happened to Evangelical Theology?* (Grand Rapids: Eerdmans, 1994).

27 This will be covered in chapter 5.

Chapter 2

28 The Docent Group, https://www.docentgroup.com; Ministry Pass, https://ministrypass.com; Lifeway Christian Resources, https://www.lifeway.com/en/articles/pastors-sermon-index-by-scripture. Sermonary, https://www.sermonary.com.

I understand that different individuals will make use of these services in more or less honorable ways, but the fact remains that the existence of these services strikes at the essence of preaching. Even more, when a sermon-building website like Sermonary trademarks the creation of "drag-and-drop sermons," it prospers from pastors who are copying and pasting the work of others. While not inherently encouraging the practice, technology has a way of aiding and abetting.

29 One of the reasons many women are entering pulpits and preaching to congregations on Sundays is because they are good communicators. And, of course, they are. God has gifted his church with biblically sound women who are gifted to teach. But possessing such a gift does not determine the use of those gifts—God's Word does. Hence, for reasons clearly articulated in 1 Timothy 2–3 and Titus 2, women are to teach women and are not permitted to teach the whole household of God. Yet such a posture requires an unfailing commitment

to the whole counsel of Scripture and the wise dictates that God prescribes for his church.

By contrast, when charismatic gifts determine the methods of ministry, all sorts of experiments will occur in church. While unsuspecting Christians might not be able to tell the difference, those with a Bible in their hands can discover that God has something to say about the order of his church. And one of the things it says is biblically qualified men—not any man, but those recognized by the congregation as qualified by God—are the ones who can teach the whole congregation.

30 If you want to see what this looks like in action, you should read about my grandfather-in-law. David Schrock, "70 Years at the Same Church: Valuable Lessons from a Persevering Pastor," *Southern Equip*, September 22, 2020, https://equip.sbts.edu/article/70-years-at-the-same-church-valuable-lessons-from-a-persevering-pastor.

31 Robert W. Yarbrough, *The Letters to Timothy and Titus* (Pillar New Testament Commentary; Grand Rapids: Eerdmans, 2018), 197.

32 David Schrock, "Where Do Elders Come From?, Via Emmaus, March 22, 2019, https://davidschrock.com/2019/03/22/where-do-elders-come-from.

33 Even children raised in church can see this. On a recent Sunday, when a retired pastor preached at our church, my seven-year-old son, seeing my absence from the pulpit, asked an important question: "But is he trained?" I do not know where this question came from, but it is one that we should be able answer in the affirmative anytime a man stands to preach.

34 Jonathan Edwards, "Resolutions," in The Works of Jonathan Edwards, vol. 1 (1834; Peabody, MA: Hendrickson, 2000), lxiii.

35 Such personal knowledge gets at the issue of congregation size, but I'll leave that for another book. For now, we can surmise that mega-churches, multi-sites, and internet "services" have changed the nature of pastoral ministry. And for those who get their ecclesiology from the Bible, that change is not a happy or healthy one.

CHAPTER 3

36 David Wells, *No Place for Truth: Whatever Happened to Evangelical Theology?* (Grand Rapids: Eerdmans, 1994), 101, 182–83.

37 Ironically, even musicians are generally obligated to provide the name of

the writer or composer who wrote the lyrics and the music. See the copyright rules at https://us.ccli.com/copyright-license. Thanks to my editor for this illuminating comparison.

38   Reading Scripture's own printed sermons (i.e., Hebrews, Ecclesiastes, or the Sermon on the Mount) might be better. Recently, our own church was forced to do this. Instead of playing a video or borrowing a sermon, we simply read the whole book of Hebrews. It was the best sermon ever preached in our pulpit.

39   Jonathan Edwards, "A Treatise Concerning Religious Affections," in *The Works of Jonathan Edwards*, vol. 2 (1834; Peabody, MA: Hendrickson, 2000), 234–343.

40   Mike Cosper, "The Rise and Fall of Mars Hill," *Christianity Today Podcast*, https://www.christianitytoday.com/ct/podcasts/rise-and-fall-of-mars-hill.

41   We will consider this further in chapter 5.

42   When someone steals something physical, the illegal transmission of property is visible to all. In the case of intellectual theft, the immaterial nature of the "property" is not visible and may not even appear to deprive the victim of anything. But this material difference does not change stealing into something permissible.

43   "'Sermongate' Prompts a Quandary: Should Pastors Borrow Words from Another?" *New York Times*, July 6, 2021, https://www.nytimes.com/2021/07/06/us/sermongate-plagiarism-litton-greear.html.

44   Ministry Pass, "Ministry Pass," YouTube, October 3, 2018, https://www.youtube.com/watch?v=_C8itYR0EP0.

45   Eugene Peterson, *The Contemplative Pastor: Returning to the Art of Spiritual Direction*, Kindle Edition (Grand Rapids: Eerdmans, 1993), Loc. 60.

46   This is John Piper's testimony after listening to the sermons of Harold J. Ockenga. I would encourage you to read how Ockenga's preaching led an unlikely speaker to become one of our generation's most powerful preachers. John Piper, *The Supremacy of God in Preaching* (Grand Rapids: Baker, 1990), 17-19. There are newer editions to this excellent book, but this first edition is the one I have and in which I read the story years ago.

CHAPTER 4

47   Ed Litton, "Pastor's Statement," Redemption Church, https://www.goredemption.com/pastors-statement.

48 "Building a Preaching Team: An Interview with Ed Litton," Sermonary, https://sermonary.co/building-a-preaching-team.

49 Ibid.

50 Ibid.

51 Ibid.

52 Marshall McLuhan, *Understanding Media: Extensions of Man, Critical Edition* (ed. Terrence Gordon; Berkeley, CA: Ginkgo Press, 1994), 17–35.

53 For the record, there are plenty of godly women who know biblical womanhood from the Bible and from lived experience. These women should teach women, just as Titus 2:5 says, and they should add their gifts, perspectives, and voices to the congregation in the way that Paul assigns in 1 Corinthians 11 and 14. My main point here is not to arbitrate the ongoing discussion about men's and women's roles. The Baptist Faith and Message 2000 has done that sufficiently. My argument aims at defending the sufficiency of Scripture. Lived experience does not override the authority, clarity, and sufficiency of God's Word.

54 I add women here because if pastors are delivering sermons with their wives and inviting women to preach Mother's Day messages, I am sure some are also building sermon teams with women.

55 The Rocket Company, https://www.therocketcompany.com/our-story.

56 The Rocket Company, "3 Secrets to Building the Best Preaching Team," YouTube, https://www.youtube.com/watch?v=tPs5_qkjIgM.

57 Ibid.

58 Hello Church, "Why a Preaching Team Makes You Better (And How to Build One)." YouTube, August 18, 2020, https://www.youtube.com/watch?v=-J1NODfRKTcs. Their full mission statement reads: "Ministry Pass is a teaching resource and multimedia service for pastors. We exist to help church leaders plan, prepare, and preach compelling sermon series." See Hello Church, YouTube, https://www.youtube.com/channel/UCQmgTUkmYXfgMKXM72KAvyw/about.

59 Ibid.

60 In our church, we regularly take our elders to Simeon Trust workshops. Simeon Trust is the ministry of David Helm, which equips preachers in solid principles of biblical exposition. We also ask aspiring teachers to learn Simeon

Trust's "First Principles" as a shared starting place for biblical interpretation and exposition.

61   Joel   Brooks,   "9   Reasons   Why   Lead   Pastors   Should Preach   Less,"   Harbor   Media,   https://www.harbormedia.com/ blog-roll/9-reasons-why-lead-pastors-should-preach-less.

62   The pressure to let women preach is directly related to this point, and many churches who are nominally complementarian are finding ways to let women assert their voice in the gathered church. This does not match the teaching of 1 Timothy 2–3, but it does fit the spirit of the age.

63   Citing Donald Guthrie, *The Pastoral Epistles* (Downers Grove, IL: InterVarsity, 1957), 31, George W. Knight, *The Pastoral Epistles: A Commentary on the Greek Text* (Grand Rapids: Eerdmans, 1992), 29, makes this point.

CHAPTER 5

64   Malcolm Gladwell, "Something Borrowed: Should a Charge of Plagiarism Ruin Your Life?" in *What the Dog Saw and Other Adventures* (New York: Little Brown and Co., 2009), 222–43.

65   Ibid., 236.

66   Throughout Charles Spurgeon's ministry we find this tension at play. In one instance, he will condemn buying sermons outright, and in another, he will make qualified exceptions for borrowing sermons. For a review of Spurgeon's sentiments and an appraisal of his views, see Geoff Chang, "'Dumb Dogs' in the Pulpit: Spurgeon on Borrowed Sermons." The Spurgeon Center, July 5, 2021, https://www.spurgeon.org/resource-library/articles/ dumb-dogs-in-the-pulpit-spurgeon-on-borrowed-sermons.

67   Gladwell, "Something Borrowed," 235.

68   At the risk of being self-referential, I would submit that the title of this book is such an example.

69   For more on the Greek philosophers, see John B. Polhill, *Acts* (New American Commentary; Nashville: Broadman & Holman, 1992), 375.

70   Gary Edward Schnittjer, *Old Testament Use of Old Testament: A Book-by-Book Guide* (Grand Rapids: Zondervan, 2021); D. A. Carson and G. K. Beale, eds., *Commentary on the New Testament Use of the Old Testament* (Grand Rapids: Baker Academic, 2007).

71   E.g., Gen. 1:3; Pss. 33:9; 147:15–18; Jer. 23:28–29; Isa. 55:10–11; and Phil 1:18.

72   Bryan Chappell, *Christ-Centered Preaching: Redeeming the Expository Sermon* (Grand Rapids: Baker, 1994), 18–19. Emphasis added.

73   See, e.g., Nicholas Piotrowski, *Matthew's New David at the End of Exile: A Socio-Rhetorical Study of Scriptural Quotations. Supplements to Novum Testamentum* (Leiden: Brill, 2016), 170. Lest you think this kind of academic monograph has no place in the pastor's study, this volume by my friend and president of Indianapolis Theological Seminary was instrumental in helping me preach Matthew 2:13–15. As I am trying to show, good preaching does depend on the work of others.

74   If we had more time, we could also follow the way Jesus cited, alluded to, and depended on Scripture. For all the disciples learned from him how to read and apply the Old Testament to him and his finished work.

75   For more on this point, see the helpful discussion between Mark Dever and Jonathan Leeman, "On Plagiarism in the Pulpit (with Ben Lacey)," Pastors Talk, July 7, 2021, https://www.9marks.org/conversations/episode-175-on-plagiarism-in-the-pulpit-with-ben-lacey.

76   G. K. Beale gives these ranges in his discussion of "Recognizing Allusions in the New Testament," in his invaluable *Handbook on the New Testament Use of the Old Testament* (Grand Rapids: Baker Academic, 2012), 31.

77   Ibid., 31.

78   I talk more about "biblical instincts" in a blog post called "How Did You See That? A Case for Scripture Saturation," Via Emmaus, October 21, 2020, https://davidschrock.com/2020/10/21/how-did-you-see-that-a-case-for-scripture-saturation.

79   Douglas Wilson, *Wordsmithy: Hot Tips for the Writing Life* (Moscow, ID: Canon, 2011), 10.

80   "The Arc of the Moral Universe Is Long, But It Bends Towards Justice," Quote Investigator, November 5, 2012, https://quoteinvestigator.com/2012/11/15/arc-of-universe. I recognize that King has also been embroiled in controversy regarding plagiarism in his academic works. The principles I am offering here do not apply to directly academic works or written material. I am focusing on the spoken word. There is a crucial difference between preaching and writing, one that I will cover when we get to annotating our sermon manuscripts.

81   Wilson, *Wordsmithy*, 109.

82 D. Martyn Lloyd-Jones, *Preaching and Preachers* (Grand Rapids: Zondervan, 1971), 158.

83 Ibid.

84 The irony of citing Douglas Wilson is that he himself has not escaped the charge of plagiarism. Only when it came to light that a book he co-authored with Randy Booth included plagiarized material, he publicly repented. "The Names on the Cover," *Blog and Mablog*, December 12, 2015, https://dougwils.com/books-and-culture/s7-engaging-the-culture/110015.html.

85 Wilson, *Wordsmithy*, 107.

86 See, e.g., J. Oswald Sanders, "The Leader and Reading," in *Spiritual Leadership: Principles of Excellence for Every Believer* (Chicago: Moody, 1994), 101–08.

87 Wilson, *Wordsmithy*, 109.

88 Ibid., 109.

89 See the back cover of John Piper, *Desiring God: Meditations of a Christian Hedonist* (Colorado Springs: Multnomah, 2003).

90 Ibid., 110.

91 Charles Spurgeon, "The Soul Winner, Or, How to Lead Sinners to the Savior" (1895); cited by Geoff Chang, "Dumb Dogs."

92 Even Spurgeon, who spoke passionately against using the sermons of others, found himself in a position where he printed the sermon of another preacher as his own. See Chang, "Dumb Dogs."

Conclusion

93 On this point, idolatry is a kind of cosmic plagiarism—using God's world without giving him proper attribution (Rom. 1:21–23).

94 As J.D. Greear put it, when defending the sharing of sermons, "I told [Ed Litton] whatever bullets of mine worked in his gun, to use them!" Scott Barkley, "Litton, Greear Say Litton Had Permission to Borrow from Sermon," *Arkansas Baptist News*, June 29, 2021, https://arkansasbaptist.org/post/litton-greear-say-litton-had-permission-to-borrow-from-sermon

95 I outlined the evidence for this cottage industry in chapter 1.

FOUNDERS
M I N I S T R I E S

Founders Ministries exists for the recovery of the gospel and the reformation of churches.

We have been providing resources for churches since 1982 through conferences, books, The Sword & The Trowel Podcast, video documentaries, online articles found at www.founders.org, the quarterly Founders Journal, Bible studies, International church search, and the seminary level training program, the Institute of Public Theology. Founders believes that the biblical faith is inherently doctrinal, and we are therefore confessional in our convictions.

You can learn more about Founders Ministries and how to partner with us at www.founders.org.

FoundersMin

FoundersMin

FoundersMinistries

FoundersMinistries

Truth & Grace Memory Books

Edited by Thomas K. Ascol

Memorizing a good, age-appropriate catechism is as
valuable for learning the Bible as memorizing multiplication tables is for learning mathematics.

—Dr. Don Whitney, Professor,
The Southern Baptist Theological Seminary

Dear Timothy: Letters on Pastoral Ministry

Edited by Thomas K. Ascol

Get this book. So many experienced pastors have written in this
book it is a gold mine of wisdom for young pastors in how to
preach and carry out their ministerial life.

—Joel Beeke, President,
Puritan Reformed Theological Seminary

The Mystery of Christ, His Covenant & His Kingdom

By Samuel Renihan

This book serves for an excellent and rich primer on covenant
theology and demonstrates how it leads from the Covenant of
Redemption to the final claiming and purifying of the people
given by the Father to the Son.

—Tom Nettles, Retired Professor of Historical Theology,
The Southern Baptist Theological Seminary